MASTER CHATGPT EFFORTLESSLY

THE SIMPLE WAY TO UNDERSTAND NATURAL LANGUAGE PROCESSING, BOOST EFFICIENCY THROUGH AUTOMATION, AND WRITE POWERFUL PROMPTS

SAMUEL THORPE

D1607436

TABLE OF CONTENTS

INTRODUCTION

In 1956, an engineer named Arthur Samuel wrote a computer program that could play checkers. It was one of the earliest examples of a machine learning to perform a task, something that would lay the groundwork for what we now call artificial intelligence. Fast forward to today, and AI has woven itself into our daily lives, from suggesting what movie to watch next to diagnosing diseases. Among these advancements, one tool stands out: ChatGPT. For many, it is a glimpse into a future where machines understand and converse with humans seamlessly.

But what is ChatGPT, really? And how can it benefit you? This book, "Mastering ChatGPT Effortlessly: The Simple Way to Understand Natural Language Processing, Boost Efficiency through Automation, and Write Powerful Prompts," seeks to answer those questions. The purpose here is straightforward: to make ChatGPT accessible to beginners and guide you in tapping into its vast potential.

The vision for this book is to be a conversation starter. It is not about getting lost in technical jargon but about understanding how ChatGPT can be applied in everyday life and work. Think of it as a guide to crafting prompts that resonate, whether you're writing a business email or exploring creative storytelling.

Who is this book for? It's for adults and teens curious about technology but who might feel overwhelmed by it. It's for those who want to explore new ways to boost efficiency in business and personal projects. It's for artists and writers looking for a new tool to unlock creativity. In essence, it's for anyone who has ever wondered how to make technology work better for them.

As we navigate this digital landscape, understanding the cultural and ethical implications of AI is crucial. This book encourages you to think critically about the role of AI in society. It urges you to consider not just what AI can do but what it should do. This is especially important as these technologies continue to evolve and integrate into our lives.

Allow me to introduce myself. I am Samuel Thorpe. My passion lies in helping people, particularly those new to technology, overcome challenges and find clarity in the ever-evolving digital world. I've spent years researching and guiding others to make technology accessible and useful.

The structure of the book is designed to guide you from the basics to more complex applications. We start with an introduction to ChatGPT, explaining what it is and how it works. As you progress, you'll find detailed and versatile prompts, exercises to practice, and applications across various fields. By the end, you'll have a toolkit to use ChatGPT effectively in your projects.

The research for this book draws from multiple sources. It includes insights from experts in AI, practical examples from everyday users, and my own experiences. This blend ensures a well-rounded perspective, offering both theoretical knowledge and actionable advice.

While the subject matter is advanced, I've made an effort to keep the tone engaging and approachable. You won't find dense technical manuals here. Instead, the goal is to make learning enjoyable, mixing advanced ideas with clear explanations. This book also includes examples, stories, and analogies to keep the content relatable. Interactive elements like quizzes offer a chance to test your knowledge as you go. These features make the book not just a read, but an experience.

In conclusion, this book is an invitation. An invitation to explore a fascinating tool that can transform the way you work and create. A call to examine the possibilities and embrace the challenges that come with new technology. I invite you to join me on this journey, to discover how ChatGPT can become an invaluable part of your toolkit. Let's explore what it means to truly understand and utilize this remarkable technology. The journey begins now.

CHAPTER 1

GETTING STARTED WITH CHATGPT

In late November 2022, a curious group of engineers at OpenAI released a seemingly innocuous tool into the wild. Its name was ChatGPT, and it carried with it modest expectations. Yet, what happened next was nothing short of a phenomenon. Within weeks, ChatGPT captured the imaginations of millions, becoming a viral success and sparking a global conversation about artificial intelligence. How does a piece of technology achieve such prominence? And more importantly, why should you care? The answers lie in understanding ChatGPT, where it came from, and what it can do for you in your daily life.

1.1 WHAT IS CHATGPT? AN OVERVIEW

To grasp the significance of ChatGPT, we must first explore its origins. OpenAI, the innovative organization behind it, was founded with a bold mission: to ensure that artificial general intelligence benefits all of humanity. This mission is not just a corporate tagline; it's a guiding principle that drives every project they undertake. From the inception of GPT-1 to the refined capabilities of GPT-3.5, ChatGPT emerges as a testament to their relentless pursuit of progress in the field of natural language processing (NLP).

The journey of ChatGPT began with GPT-1, which laid the foundation for understanding language patterns. It was soon followed by GPT-2, a model that astonished researchers with its ability to generate coherent text. However, it was GPT-3, released in 2020, that truly pushed the boundaries. GPT-3.5, the backbone of Chat-GPT, builds on this legacy with enhanced capabilities and refined algorithms. Each iteration marks a significant leap forward, bringing us closer to machines that can genuinely understand and respond to human language in meaningful ways. ChatGPT represents the culmination of these advancements, a fine-tuned marvel poised to engage with users in more nuanced and sophisticated interactions.

The core functionalities of ChatGPT are what make it truly remarkable. At its heart, ChatGPT excels in generating human-like text. Whether you're composing an email, crafting a story, or brainstorming ideas, ChatGPT can assist with a level of fluency that feels natural. It's also adept at answering questions and providing insights and information on a wide range of topics. Beyond mere text generation, ChatGPT engages in conversation, responding to prompts with contextually relevant replies. This conversational prowess allows it to simulate dialogue and even perform specific tasks based on carefully crafted prompts. In essence, ChatGPT operates as a digital assistant, poised to augment your capabilities in both mundane and creative endeavors.

The technology powering ChatGPT is both complex and fascinating, yet it can be understood in simpler terms. At its core lies the Transformer model, a groundbreaking architecture in NLP that uses a mechanism called self-attention. This allows ChatGPT to weigh the importance of different words in a sentence, leading to more accurate and context-aware text generation. The process begins with pre-training, where the model learns from vast datasets, followed by fine-tuning, which refines its capabilities based on specific tasks. Tokenization, another key aspect, involves breaking down text into manageable pieces, enabling the model to generate coherent and cohesive responses.

Despite its impressive capabilities, ChatGPT has limitations. Its strength lies in content generation, where it can produce high-quality text rapidly. However, it sometimes struggles with understanding complex contexts, leading to less accurate responses. Additionally, ethical considerations must be taken into account. ChatGPT, like all AI models, can inadvertently perpetuate biases present in its training data. OpenAI acknowledges these challenges, consistently working to improve the model's accuracy and fairness.

As you explore ChatGPT further, it becomes clear that while it is a powerful tool, it is not infallible. It requires thoughtful prompts and careful consideration of its outputs. Yet, its potential is undeniable, offering a glimpse into a future where technology and human creativity converge in unprecedented ways.

1.2 SETTING UP YOUR CHATGPT ACCOUNT

Creating a ChatGPT account is your first step towards unlocking a world of possibilities with AI. You begin this process by visiting the OpenAI website. Upon reaching the website, you'll find a straightforward layout guiding you to the registration section. Here, you can create an account using your email address or through third-party options like Google, Microsoft, or Apple. The choice is yours, but using a personal email is often recommended for ease of access. Once you've entered your details, OpenAI will send you a verification email. It's a simple step, yet crucial, as it ensures that your account is secure and that you are the rightful owner. Look for the email in your inbox, and click the verification link. This action will confirm your account and grant you access to the ChatGPT environment.

Upon setting up your account, you will encounter various access levels and subscription options. OpenAI provides a free tier, which is perfect for getting acquainted with ChatGPT's basic functionalities. This tier allows you to explore the platform without any financial commitment, offering a range of features that cater to casual users. However, for those seeking enhanced capabilities, there is the ChatGPT Plus subscription, which is priced at a monthly rate. This premium option comes with benefits such as faster response times and priority access, making it ideal for users who rely heavily on the tool for professional or frequent use. Considering the cost against the value it provides, many find the premium features well worth the investment, especially if they use ChatGPT for business or creative projects.

Once your account is verified and you've chosen your subscription plan, the next step involves configuring your settings to optimize your ChatGPT experience. Start by setting your preferences, which allows you to tailor the interface and functionality to your liking. You can adjust notification settings to ensure you only receive alerts relevant to you. This customization helps in managing information flow and prevents unnecessary distractions. Additionally, understanding privacy settings is paramount. These settings control what information you share with OpenAI and how your data is handled, allowing you to use ChatGPT confidently and knowing your privacy is respected.

With your settings configured, it's time to familiarize yourself with the user dashboard. The dashboard is your control center, where you'll find all the tools and features ChatGPT offers. The navigation menu is intuitive, providing easy access to different sections of the platform. Here, you can initiate new chats, explore settings, or review past interactions. Key features are prominently displayed, making it simple for you to utilize ChatGPT's capabilities efficiently. Additionally, the dashboard includes links to help and support resources. These resources are invaluable, especially when you encounter questions or require further guidance on specific functionalities.

Interactive Element: Quick Start Checklist

- Visit the OpenAI website and navigate to the registration section.
- Create an account using your preferred method (email, Google, etc.).
- Verify your account via the email link sent by OpenAI.
- Choose between the free tier or ChatGPT Plus subscription.
- Configure your account settings, including preferences and privacy.
- Explore the user dashboard, familiarizing yourself with key features.

The journey of setting up a ChatGPT account is not merely about logging in; it's about creating a tailored experience that aligns with your needs and preferences. Each step, from verification to exploring the dashboard, is designed to empower you to make the most of this remarkable tool. With your account ready, you are now poised to explore the expansive world of possibilities that ChatGPT offers.

1.3 NAVIGATING THE CHATGPT INTERFACE

Engaging with ChatGPT begins with understanding its user interface, a space designed to facilitate clear and efficient interaction. At the center of this digital realm lies the main chat window, the heart of your conversations. This area displays the ongoing dialogue, where your prompts appear alongside ChatGPT's responses. It's the dynamic canvas where creativity and inquiry unfold, providing a seamless flow of interaction that mimics face-to-face communication. To the side, the sidebar navigation offers a gateway to different functionalities, keeping you oriented as you explore. This section houses shortcuts to your chat history, allowing you to revisit past exchanges, as well as links to settings and support. The sidebar serves as your compass, guiding you through the landscape of options available at your fingertips. Below the chat window, the input and output sections are where the magic happens. You type your prompts here, and ChatGPT's responses materialize in the output, a space that adapts to your inquiries with remarkable fluency.

Interactivity is a cornerstone of the ChatGPT experience, and the interface reflects this through various features. The toolbar, positioned strategically, offers functionalities that enhance your usage. Here, you can access options to adjust the session, clear the conversation, or export the chat for future reference. These tools are designed to streamline your workflow, providing quick solutions to common needs. Shortcut commands further augment this efficiency. By learning a few simple keystrokes, you can navigate the interface with ease, whether it's initiating a new conversation or switching themes. Another valuable asset is the help icon, a small but mighty tool that connects you to a wealth of resources. Clicking it opens a portal to guides, FAQs, and troubleshooting tips, ensuring that assistance is always within reach when you encounter a challenge or have a question.

Personalization is key to making ChatGPT truly yours, and the interface offers several ways to tailor your environment. One of the most immediate changes you can make is switching between light and dark modes, adjusting the theme to match your preference or reduce eye strain. This simple toggle can transform your interaction space, making it more comfortable for extended use. Additionally, you can adjust text size and font, ensuring that the display aligns with your reading habits and visual needs. Configuring layout settings allows for further customization. You can choose how elements are arranged, optimizing the interface for your workflow and ensuring that the tools you use most frequently are readily accessible.

For those who seek a deeper level of control, the command line offers an intriguing avenue. This feature, often associated with more advanced users, provides a direct method to execute specific operations and access settings beyond the standard interface. Basic command line operations include running scripts and executing commands that automate tasks or retrieve detailed information. This functionality can be handy for users who wish to integrate ChatGPT into larger projects or systems. By accessing advanced settings via the command line, you can tap into features that offer greater precision and customization, perfect for tailoring the tool to specialized needs. This level of control empowers you to mold ChatGPT into a versatile assistant that responds to your queries and adapts to your unique workflow and requirements.

By understanding and leveraging these interface elements, you position yourself to interact with ChatGPT in ways that maximize its potential. Whether crafting an intricate query or simply exploring the tool's capabilities, the interface serves as your guide and canvas, ready to adapt to your needs and enhance your experience.

1.4 BASIC COMMANDS AND INTERACTIONS

Understanding the basic commands of ChatGPT is akin to learning the fundamental tools in a new language. These are your building blocks, the starting point from which you can explore the vast landscape of possibilities this AI offers. Begin with asking questions. This command is straightforward yet powerful. You type a question, and ChatGPT responds with an answer. Whether you're seeking information on a historical event or the meaning of a word, this function is your gateway to acquiring knowledge. Think of it as having a digital encyclopedia at your fingertips, ready to provide insights with just a few keystrokes. Generating text is another core function. Here, you provide a prompt, and ChatGPT produces a coherent piece of text. This is particularly useful for tasks like writing essays, crafting stories, or even drafting messages. It's like having a skilled writer on standby, ready to assist with your creative and professional needs. Additionally, you can request summaries. This function distills lengthy articles or reports into concise summaries, saving you time and effort. It's perfect for when you're short on time but need to grasp the essence of a document. Finally, ChatGPT can translate text, opening up a world of communication across languages. This feature is invaluable for those engaged in international correspondence or simply curious about different languages.

Interactive conversations with ChatGPT are where the tool truly shines. Initiating dialogue is as simple as typing a greeting or a question. The AI responds, and thus a conversation begins. What sets ChatGPT apart is its ability to follow up on previous exchanges, creating a dynamic and engaging interaction. This isn't just a static question-and-answer session; it's an evolving dialogue that adapts to the context you provide. For instance, imagine you're brainstorming ideas for a project. You pose a question, receive a response, and then build on that response with further inquiries. ChatGPT keeps track of the conversation's flow, allowing for a more natural and intuitive exchange. This capability enhances its utility as a brainstorming partner or a sounding board for ideas. You can refine the interaction by using conversational context, making it more relevant and targeted. It's like having a conversation with a knowledgeable colleague, where each response builds on the previous one, leading to deeper insights and understanding.

When it comes to task-specific commands, ChatGPT proves itself to be a versatile assistant. Writing emails is one such task. You can provide a brief outline of what you wish to convey, and ChatGPT can draft a professional email for you. This feature is a time-saver and helps ensure clarity and professionalism in your communication. Creating lists is another practical application. Whether it's a to-do list, a grocery list, or a list of potential project ideas, ChatGPT can organize your thoughts into structured formats. Drafting reports is yet another area in which ChatGPT excels. Provide the necessary data points and context, and it can help compile these into a coherent report, complete with sections, headings, and conclusions. These task-specific commands transform ChatGPT into a multi-functional tool capable of assisting with a wide range of professional and personal tasks.

Despite its capabilities, using ChatGPT effectively hinges on understanding its limitations and best practices. Clear and concise prompts are crucial for obtaining accurate and helpful responses. When your input is straightforward and unambiguous, ChatGPT can more easily comprehend and generate relevant outputs. Avoiding ambiguous language is equally important. Vague or complex phrasing can confuse the AI, leading to less accurate responses. Instead, aim for simplicity and precision in your prompts. Also, don't hesitate to iterate on prompts for better results. Sometimes, the first response might be different from what you need, and refining your input can yield improved outcomes. This process of iteration is akin to refining your questions in a conversation to extract more information from a knowledgeable source. By embracing these best practices, you can maximize the effectiveness of ChatGPT, turning it into a reliable and invaluable tool in your digital toolkit.

1.5 TROUBLESHOOTING COMMON SETUP ISSUES

Setting up ChatGPT should be a straightforward process, but like all things digital, it sometimes comes with hiccups. One of the most frequent challenges users face is account verification failures. Imagine eagerly setting up your account, only to find that the verification email never arrives. This can happen for several reasons, such as the email landing in your spam folder or a typo in your email address during the registration process. It's a simple oversight, but it can stall your progress. Another common issue is connectivity problems, particularly if you're in an area with spotty internet service. A stable internet connection is crucial for interacting with ChatGPT, as any interruptions can disrupt the flow of information. Subscription and billing issues also arise, especially when users accidentally select the wrong plan or encounter errors during payment processing. It's frustrating to be ready to explore ChatGPT's features only to find that a billing issue stands in your way.

Now, let's address these problems with some practical solutions. If you're facing account verification failures, the first step is to check your spam or junk folder, as verification emails sometimes get diverted there. If that doesn't work, resending the verification email is your best bet. Most platforms, including ChatGPT, offer an option to resend verification emails on their login or sign-up page. For connectivity issues, ensure that your internet connection is stable. You can do this by checking your router and restarting it if necessary. Sometimes, simply switching to a different network or using a wired connection can solve the problem. For subscription and billing concerns, contacting OpenAI's support team is advisable. They can provide guidance on resolving payment errors or adjusting your subscription plan to align with your needs. Having your account details and any error messages ready will help the support team assist you more efficiently.

Knowing where to find help can make all the difference when you encounter difficulties. OpenAI offers a range of support resources that you can access with ease. The OpenAI support center is a comprehensive hub for troubleshooting guides, offering step-by-step solutions to common issues. It's your first stop when things go awry. Community forums are another invaluable resource, providing a platform where users share experiences and solutions. Engaging with the community can offer insights into how others have resolved similar problems, and you may find answers to questions you hadn't thought of asking. The Frequently Asked Questions (FAQs) section is a trove of information covering everything from account setup to advanced features. Browsing through the FAQs can preemptively address concerns and enhance your understanding of ChatGPT's functionalities.

Prevention, as they say, is better than cure. By taking proactive steps, you can minimize the likelihood of encountering setup issues in the first place. Keep your software updated to ensure compatibility with the latest features and security protocols. Regular updates not only enhance performance but also resolve known bugs and glitches. Employ strong passwords to protect your account from unauthorized access. A combination of letters, numbers, and special characters makes for a robust password. It's a simple measure that goes a long way in safeguarding your digital presence. Regularly reviewing your account settings is also beneficial. It allows you to confirm that your preferences, notifications, and privacy settings are aligned with your intentions. This habit keeps your account streamlined and reduces the possibility of unexpected disruptions.

In the dynamic world of technology, challenges are inevitable. However, with the right tools and mindset, they become manageable. Each step you take to troubleshoot or prevent issues is an investment in a smoother, more efficient experience with Chat-GPT. By being prepared, you can navigate these challenges with confidence, ensuring that your interaction with this powerful tool remains seamless and productive.

1.6 ETHICAL CONSIDERATIONS IN AI USAGE

As we delve deeper into the realm of artificial intelligence, the ethical implications of tools like ChatGPT become increasingly important. These concerns aren't just theoretical—they affect real-world applications and decisions. Privacy sits at the forefront of these issues. With AI systems handling vast amounts of personal data, the risk of breaches looms large. Users may wonder how their information is stored and used, and rightfully so. Data security is critical, as any vulnerability can lead to unauthorized access or misuse. Such breaches not only compromise individual privacy but also erode trust in technology. Equally significant is the potential for bias in AI responses. These systems learn from existing data, and if that data reflects societal biases, AI outputs might unintentionally perpetuate them. This can manifest in various ways, from skewed information dissemination to reinforcing stereotypes.

Using ChatGPT responsibly involves several key practices. First, respecting user privacy is paramount. Always be conscious of the data shared with AI systems, and ensure that interactions are limited to non-sensitive information whenever possible. This approach minimizes exposure risks and promotes user confidence. Another critical aspect is avoiding the misuse of AI-generated content. With great power comes great responsibility, and using AI outputs ethically is essential. Whether crafting content or generating ideas, the intention should always align with honesty and integrity. Transparency in AI interactions fosters trust and understanding. Users should be aware of AI capabilities and limitations, preventing misconceptions about what these systems can and cannot do.

Fairness in AI applications is not a luxury but a necessity. Addressing biases involves actively working to minimize them in AI outputs. Diverse training data is vital, as it broadens the context and reduces the likelihood of skewed results. Diverse data ensures that AI systems reflect a more comprehensive view of society, capturing the nuances and variations that exist. Encouraging equitable AI practices means going beyond mere functionality; it requires a commitment to inclusivity and fair representation across all AI applications. This commitment must be reflected in the design, testing, and deployment of AI systems.

Structured frameworks and standards have been established to guide ethical AI usage. OpenAI, for instance, has developed ethical guidelines that outline best practices and principles for AI development and deployment. These guidelines serve as a roadmap, ensuring that AI systems are used in a manner that upholds ethical standards. Industry standards and best practices also play a crucial role, providing a foundation for organizations to build upon as they implement AI solutions. Case studies of ethical AI deployment offer valuable insights, showcasing how ethical considerations can be integrated into real-world applications. These examples highlight the positive impact of aligning AI usage with ethical principles, demonstrating the potential for AI to be a force for good when managed responsibly.

In considering these ethical dimensions, the goal is to ensure that AI remains a tool for empowerment and progress. It should be a catalyst for innovation, not a source of inequality or harm. As we continue exploring AI's potential, we are responsible for navigating these ethical complexities with care and foresight. By prioritizing ethical considerations, we can embrace AI's benefits while safeguarding against its potential pitfalls. In doing so, we not only enhance the technology itself but also pave the way for a more equitable and transparent digital future.

CHAPTER 2
WRITING EFFECTIVE PROMPTS

Imagine standing at the door of a grand library. The shelves are brimming with endless volumes, each one eager to share its tales and knowledge. Yet, to unlock these treasures, you need the right key—a prompt. In the realm of ChatGPT, your prompt is that key. It is not merely an input but the foundation of a dialogue between you and the AI, setting the stage for the responses you receive. Understanding prompts is crucial, as they guide the AI in generating relevant and meaningful content. This chapter will explore what makes a prompt effective, how to craft one, and why it matters.

A prompt is your initial input text to the AI—a question, a directive, or a request. It's the seed from which the AI draws its responses. Think of it as a conversation starter, a way to engage with ChatGPT's capabilities. The prompt serves as the basis for generating responses and determining the direction and depth of the AI's output. This process mirrors a dialogue, where the clarity and specificity of your words shape the conversation's course. Just as a well-phrased question can elicit a thoughtful answer from a friend, a carefully crafted prompt can draw out insightful and precise responses from ChatGPT.

The importance of a good prompt cannot be overstated. A well-crafted prompt is essential for obtaining accurate and useful responses. Clarity in communication is paramount; it reduces ambiguity and ensures that the AI understands your intent. A clear prompt is like giving someone a map with a precise route, rather than vague directions. This precision enhances the relevance of answers, allowing ChatGPT to provide information that aligns with your needs. A prompt that clearly articulates the task at hand helps the AI focus its resources on producing the most appropriate response, thereby improving the overall quality of the interaction.

Prompts come in various forms, each serving a unique purpose. Open-ended questions invite expansive answers, encouraging the AI to explore different angles and possibilities. These prompts are ideal for brainstorming or when seeking comprehensive insights. Specific task requests, on the other hand, are more focused. They direct the AI to perform a particular action, whether it's composing an email or summarizing an article. These prompts are precise, targeting a clear outcome. Contextual prompts provide background information or set the scene for the AI, helping it generate relevant and tailored responses to your situation. Each type of prompt has its place, and understanding when to use each one is key to effective communication with ChatGPT.

The prompt-response cycle is the engine that drives the interaction with ChatGPT. It begins with you inputting a prompt and setting the stage for the AI to process and generate a response. This cycle is dynamic, with each step influencing the next. ChatGPT analyzes your input, drawing on its vast knowledge base to craft a reply that aims to meet your needs. Once the AI generates a response, the cycle enters the evaluation phase. Here, you assess the accuracy and usefulness of the answer, using this feedback to refine future prompts. This iterative process is akin to a conversation, where each exchange builds on the previous one, leading to a richer and more informed dialogue.

Interactive Element: Prompt Evaluation Checklist

- **Clarity**: Is the prompt clear and unambiguous?
- **Relevance**: Does the response align with your expectations?
- **Specificity**: Is the task or question precisely defined?
- **Context**: Have you provided enough background information?
- **Outcome**: Does the response meet your needs or require refinement?

Understanding prompts is an essential skill for anyone looking to engage effectively with ChatGPT. The ability to craft and refine prompts opens up a world of possibilities, transforming the tool from a simple novelty into a valuable resource. As you explore the nuances of prompt writing, you'll discover the power of clear communication and its impact on the quality of AI interactions.

2.1 CRAFTING CLEAR AND CONCISE PROMPTS

Imagine trying to have a conversation with someone who speaks in riddles or uses overly complex language. You'd likely find it frustrating and confusing. The same principle applies when you're crafting prompts for ChatGPT. Clarity is your best ally. A clear prompt uses simple and direct language, devoid of unnecessary jargon or convoluted terms. This simplicity ensures that ChatGPT understands exactly what you're asking, leading to more precise responses. When you eliminate ambiguity, you're essentially paving a direct path for the AI to follow. It's like giving directions with clear street names instead of vague landmarks. The more straightforward your prompt, the more likely you are to receive useful and accurate information in return.

Being specific in your prompts is another key to unlocking the full potential of ChatGPT. Specificity provides the AI with a detailed map, guiding it to deliver the precise information you seek. This means including all necessary details—such as dates, locations, or other relevant specifics—within your prompt. For instance, asking "Tell me about the weather" is quite broad, but adding specifics like "What's the weather like in New York on March 12th?" gives ChatGPT the context it needs to provide a focused answer. By honing in on the specifics, you not only make it easier for ChatGPT to understand your request but also enhance the relevance and usefulness of the response it generates.

It's easy to fall into the trap of asking overly broad questions, hoping to cover all the bases in one go. However, this often leads to general or unfocused responses that may not meet your needs. Limiting the scope of your prompts helps to avoid this pitfall. Think of it as narrowing the lens through which the AI views your question. Instead of asking a sweeping question encompassing multiple themes, break down your query into smaller, more manageable parts. This approach is akin to solving a puzzle one piece at a time rather than trying to see the whole picture at once. Focusing on one aspect at a time allows ChatGPT to provide more targeted and meaningful insights.

Grammar and punctuation might seem like minor details, but they are crucial in prompt crafting. Proper grammar ensures that your prompts are structured in a way that ChatGPT can easily interpret. Imagine reading a sentence without any punctuation—it can quickly become a confusing jumble of words. Similarly, punctuation clarifies meaning, guiding the AI on how to process your request. It acts as a roadmap, indicating where one thought ends and another begins. Ensuring that your prompts are grammatically sound and punctuated correctly reduces the risk of misinterpretation, thus improving the quality of the AI's responses.

When you combine all these elements—clarity, specificity, focus, and proper grammar—you create a prompt that ChatGPT can engage with effectively. This combination transforms your interaction from a guessing game into a precise and productive exchange. As you refine your approach, you'll find that the AI becomes a more reliable partner, capable of assisting you in a multitude of tasks with greater accuracy and depth. The key is in the details, and by paying attention to how you frame your prompts, you unlock a world of possibilities with ChatGPT.

2.2 EXAMPLES OF EFFECTIVE PROMPTS FOR BEGINNERS

When you're just getting started with ChatGPT, simple prompts are your best friends. They serve as straightforward introductions to the capabilities of this tool, allowing you to quickly grasp how it functions. For instance, asking, "What is the weather like today?" is a direct and uncomplicated query. It teaches you how the AI retrieves current information and responds with relevant data. Similarly, a light-hearted prompt like "Tell me a joke" illustrates the AI's ability to generate creative and humorous content. These prompts are easy to understand and offer immediate feedback, making them perfect for beginners who want to explore ChatGPT's basic functionalities without diving into complex instructions.

Moving beyond the basics, context-based prompts add depth and richness to your interactions with ChatGPT. By providing context, you give the AI a framework within which to operate, leading to more nuanced and tailored responses. Take, for example, the prompt, "Explain the water cycle to a 10-year-old." Here, you specify not only the topic but also the complexity level appropriate for a young audience. This added context helps ChatGPT adjust its language and explanations to suit the intended reader. Similarly, asking the AI to "Summarize the plot of 'To Kill a Mockingbird'" provides it with a straightforward task and context, guiding it to deliver a concise yet informative response. These prompts demonstrate how context can transform a generic query into a precise and insightful exchange, enhancing your understanding of ChatGPT's versatility.

When you're looking for ChatGPT to perform specific tasks, task-specific prompts come into play. These prompts provide clear directives, enabling you to leverage ChatGPT's capabilities for practical applications. For instance, you might ask, "Write a professional email to a client." This prompt instructs ChatGPT to focus on crafting a formal communication, allowing you to see how it can assist in business-related tasks. Another example is "Generate a list of healthy dinner recipes," which showcases the AI's ability to compile information from various sources to meet your culinary needs. Task-specific prompts are particularly useful for those with clear objectives and want to see how ChatGPT can streamline their workflow or enhance their productivity through automation.

Iterative prompts are an excellent way to refine your inquiries and gain deeper insights. They involve a process of continual improvement, where you adjust your prompts based on the initial responses you receive. For example, if you ask, "What are the top tourist attractions in Paris?" and find the response too broad, you can refine it by specifying, "What are the top tourist attractions in Paris for art lovers?" This iterative approach allows you to hone in on the exact information you need, teaching ChatGPT to respond with more precision over time. As you iterate, you'll notice that the AI becomes more attuned to your specific preferences and requirements, leading to increasingly relevant and valuable interactions. This process not only improves the quality of the responses but also enhances your skills in crafting effective prompts, empowering you to unlock the full potential of ChatGPT in various contexts.

2.3 COMMON MISTAKES TO AVOID IN PROMPT WRITING

When interacting with ChatGPT, clarity is your ally. One of the most common pitfalls in prompt writing is ambiguity. Imagine asking someone, "Can you help?" without specifying what kind of help you need. Such a vague prompt can lead to confusion and irrelevant responses from ChatGPT. For instance, a prompt like "Tell me about the weather" could yield a broad range of information unless you specify a location or date. To clarify ambiguous prompts, focus on the details. Instead of saying, "Tell me about the weather," try, "What's the weather forecast for tomorrow in San Francisco?" By adding specificity, you guide the AI to deliver a response that aligns closely with your expectations. This specificity transforms a general query into a targeted request, significantly enhancing the quality of the interaction.

Overloading prompts with multiple requests is another mistake that can hinder effective communication with ChatGPT. Consider a scenario where you're asking, "Can you tell me about the weather in Paris, the history of the Eiffel Tower, and the best French cuisine?" Such a prompt is overloaded and can overwhelm the AI, leading to fragmented or incomplete responses. The key is to break down complex prompts into simpler, manageable parts. You could start by asking about the weather, then inquire separately about the Eiffel Tower, and finally explore French cuisine. This approach makes each prompt more digestible and allows you to obtain detailed responses for each specific question. By simplifying your requests, you enable ChatGPT to focus on one task at a time, fostering clearer and more coherent outputs.

Neglecting to provide context is another challenge that can lead to unsatisfactory results. Imagine walking into a conversation halfway through and trying to contribute without knowing the background. Prompts that lack context leave ChatGPT guessing at your intentions, often resulting in generic or off-target responses. For example, asking "Why is it important?" without any context could leave the AI grasping at straws. To improve accuracy, always provide sufficient background information. Instead of a context-less prompt, you might say, "Why is it important for students to learn coding in today's digital age?" By embedding context, you arm ChatGPT with the necessary information to tailor its responses to your specific needs. This simple addition can dramatically improve the relevance and depth of the answers you receive.

Ignoring feedback from the AI is a missed opportunity to refine your prompts. ChatGPT's responses are a reflection of your input, and paying attention to these outputs can reveal patterns and areas for improvement. If the AI consistently misinterprets your queries, it might be time to adjust your prompt structure. Consider an iterative approach: begin with a basic prompt, evaluate the response, and refine the prompt based on what you receive. Suppose your initial question about historical events yields an answer that is too broad. In that case, you could narrow it down by specifying a particular era or event. This iterative process helps you fine-tune your prompts, leading to more precise and satisfactory interactions. Recognizing the nuances in AI responses and adapting your prompts accordingly can unlock a more effective and rewarding experience with ChatGPT.

2.4 ADVANCED PROMPT STRUCTURING TECHNIQUES

When you think about crafting prompts, consider it an art that combines creativity and precision. One powerful technique you can use is incorporating conditional statements. Imagine setting up an "if-then" scenario to guide ChatGPT through a decision-making process. For instance, you might prompt it with, "If the weather is sunny, suggest outdoor activities; if it's rainy, recommend indoor pastimes." This approach helps get targeted responses and enables the AI to handle multiple potential outcomes. Similarly, multiple-choice prompts can streamline interactions, offering predefined options that guide ChatGPT to a specific area of focus. For a project, you might say, "Choose the best marketing strategy: A) Social Media, B) Email Campaign, C) Influencer Partnership." This can simplify decision-making, especially when you're juggling complex options and need quick, precise answers.

Layering prompts is another technique that can take your interactions with ChatGPT to a new level. Think of it as building a narrative, one question leading to the next, each deepening the context and enhancing the detail of the responses. Sequential questioning involves asking a series of related questions that build on each other, like peeling layers off an onion to get to the core. You might start by asking, "What are the benefits of exercise?" followed by, "How does it improve mental health?" and then, "What are some effective routines for beginners?" This layered approach allows you to explore a topic comprehensively, encouraging the AI to provide more detailed and contextually rich answers. It's beneficial when you're tackling complex subjects that require nuanced understanding.

Embedding specific instructions within your prompts can also refine the responses you receive. This method involves clearly stating the format or constraints you desire. For example, instruct ChatGPT to "Provide a summary in 50 words" or "List three benefits of a plant-based diet." By embedding these instructions, you set clear boundaries for the AI, ensuring it delivers information in the exact form you need. It's like giving a painter a canvas and a specific color palette; the artist can still be creative, but there's a framework to guide the creation. This technique is especially effective when you need concise and structured information, whether for reports, presentations, or personal projects.

Balancing open-ended and close-ended prompts is critical to maximizing the utility of ChatGPT. Open-ended prompts invite exploration and creativity, allowing the AI to expand on ideas without constraints. They are ideal when you're seeking inspiration or brainstorming, such as asking, "How can technology improve education?" This can lead to a wide range of perspectives and insights. On the other hand, close-ended prompts are more focused, often requiring a straightforward answer. They are useful for fact-checking or when you need a specific piece of information, such as, "Is the capital of France Paris?" Balancing these two types of prompts allows you to harness the full spectrum of ChatGPT's capabilities, from generating broad ideas to pinpointing exact information.

Understanding and applying these advanced techniques can significantly enhance your interactions with ChatGPT. Each method offers a unique way to engage with the AI, providing you with the tools to tailor responses to your specific needs. Whether you're exploring a topic in-depth or seeking quick, accurate answers, these strategies can help you make the most of ChatGPT's potential, turning it into an indispensable tool in your digital toolkit.

2.5 CUSTOMIZING PROMPTS FOR SPECIFIC TASKS

Tailoring prompts to suit different tasks is like choosing the right tool for a job. Each prompt should be crafted with its purpose in mind, allowing ChatGPT to deliver relevant and precise responses. Let's explore how to customize prompts for various tasks, starting with content creation.

When it comes to writing articles, blogs, or social media posts, clarity and engagement are key. Consider a prompt such as, "Draft a blog post on the benefits of remote work." This prompt guides ChatGPT to focus on a well-defined topic, encouraging it to explore various angles like productivity, work-life balance, and environmental impact. Similarly, crafting a social media caption, such as "Create a social media caption for a summer sale," requires brevity and appeal to capture the audience's attention. These prompts should inspire creativity while maintaining a clear focus, ensuring that the content aligns with your intended message and audience.

In the business world, prompts play a crucial role in streamlining communication and decision-making processes. For instance, "Generate a market analysis report" directs ChatGPT to compile data and insights into a structured format, providing valuable information for strategic planning. The AI can sift through trends and statistics, offering a comprehensive overview that aids in making informed business decisions. Meanwhile, prompts like "Write an email response to a customer complaint" require a balance of professionalism and empathy. Here, ChatGPT can assist in drafting a response that addresses the customer's concerns while maintaining a positive tone, ensuring the communication is both effective and courteous.

Educational prompts serve as powerful tools for learning and teaching. When you ask ChatGPT to "Explain the Pythagorean theorem," you're tapping into its ability to simplify complex concepts into understandable explanations. This can be incredibly helpful for students who need clear and concise information. Similarly, a prompt such as "Create a study guide for World War II history" allows the AI to organize key events and figures into a coherent format that facilitates study and retention. These prompts are designed to support educational goals, providing learners with resources that enhance their understanding and engagement with the material.

Creativity knows no bounds, and neither should your prompts for artistic endeavors. A prompt like "Write a short story about a space adventure" invites ChatGPT to tap into its storytelling capabilities, weaving narratives that capture imagination and intrigue. This can be an excellent exercise for aspiring writers looking to explore new genres or themes. Similarly, "Generate a prompt for a digital art project" can spark inspiration for artists seeking fresh ideas. The AI can suggest themes, concepts, or even specific techniques, providing a springboard for creativity that artists can adapt and build upon.

By customizing prompts to fit specific tasks, you can unlock Chat-GPT's full potential, transforming it from a general tool into a specialized assistant tailored to your needs. Whether crafting content, conducting business, learning new concepts, or exploring creative projects, the right prompt can make all the difference. As you develop this skill, you'll find that your interactions with ChatGPT become more productive and rewarding, opening up new possibilities for innovation and growth.

As we conclude this chapter, remember that prompts are not just inputs, but bridges to more meaningful and effective interactions with ChatGPT. By tailoring them to your specific needs, you create opportunities for the AI to assist you in ways that are both insightful and practical. Next, we'll explore the practical applications of these prompts in daily life, showing you how to integrate ChatGPT into your routines for enhanced productivity and creativity.

CHAPTER 3
PRACTICAL APPLICATIONS IN DAILY LIFE

I magine waking up to a perfectly organized day, where tasks align seamlessly with your goals, and productivity flows effortlessly. This is not a distant dream but a reality made possible with ChatGPT. As a digital assistant, ChatGPT offers more than just answers; it provides a structured approach to daily life, making it a powerful ally in personal productivity. Whether you're a student juggling assignments or a professional managing multiple projects, ChatGPT's capabilities can simplify your routine and enhance your efficiency. Let's explore how it transforms everyday tasks into streamlined processes, ensuring you make the most of each day.

3.1 USING CHATGPT FOR PERSONAL PRODUCTIVITY

To begin, consider task management, a vital component for maintaining order and reducing stress. ChatGPT helps you craft daily to-do lists, ensuring nothing slips through the cracks. Imagine asking, "Create a to-do list for today with tasks like grocery shopping, replying to emails, and preparing a presentation." The AI swiftly organizes your tasks, prioritizing them based on urgency and relevance. This structured approach not only clarifies your day but also boosts productivity by minimizing decision fatigue. With ChatGPT, setting up a weekly schedule becomes a breeze. It assists in allocating time blocks for work, exercise, and relaxation, promoting a balanced lifestyle. By integrating these tasks into a cohesive plan, you regain control over your time, paving the way for a more focused and fulfilling day.

Goal setting and tracking are crucial for personal growth, and ChatGPT excels in this area. It guides you in establishing SMART goals—specific, measurable, achievable, relevant, and time-bound —ensuring your objectives are clear and attainable. For instance, when you ask, "Help me set SMART goals for my fitness routine," ChatGPT provides tailored recommendations based on your current fitness level and aspirations. Additionally, it tracks your progress, offering insights on milestones achieved and areas needing improvement. Suppose your target is to finish twelve books this year; ChatGPT can monitor your reading habits, reminding you to stay on track and celebrating your achievements as you reach each goal.

Time management is another domain in which ChatGPT offers valuable insights. Suggesting productivity tips for various scenarios empowers you to work smarter, not harder. If you're working from home, you might ask, "Give me productivity tips for working from home." ChatGPT responds with strategies like setting boundaries, creating a dedicated workspace, and scheduling regular breaks to maintain focus. Moreover, it provides techniques to combat procrastination, such as breaking tasks into smaller, manageable parts and setting deadlines to create a sense of urgency. By incorporating these strategies, you optimize your workflow and enhance your ability to meet deadlines.

Automating repetitive tasks is one of ChatGPT's standout features, saving you time and effort on mundane activities. Imagine asking it to "Draft a daily journal entry summarizing my activities and reflections." ChatGPT compiles your day's events into a coherent narrative, allowing you to focus on more pressing matters. Similarly, it generates email templates for routine correspondence, streamlining communication and ensuring consistency in your messages. This automation increases your efficiency and frees up mental space for more creative and strategic tasks, enabling you to concentrate on activities that truly matter. With ChatGPT, the monotony of repetitive tasks fades away, replaced by a sense of accomplishment and forward momentum.

Interactive Element: Daily Productivity Checklist

- **Create a To-Do List**: Use ChatGPT to outline daily tasks and prioritize based on urgency.
- **Set SMART Goals**: Define specific, measurable, achievable, relevant, and time-bound objectives.
- **Track Progress**: Monitor achievements and adjust strategies as needed.
- **Automate Routine Tasks**: Streamline activities like journaling and email drafting.

ChatGPT's integration into your daily life transforms how you manage time and achieve goals. By leveraging its capabilities, you streamline tasks, enhance productivity, and create a balanced lifestyle. This AI tool becomes a personal productivity coach, guiding you through the complexities of modern life with ease and efficiency.

3.2 ENHANCING DAILY COMMUNICATION WITH CHATGPT

In today's fast-paced world, effective communication is more critical than ever. Whether you're coordinating with colleagues, reaching out to friends, or engaging with an online audience, ChatGPT can be your secret weapon. Imagine needing to send a professional email to a client. You want to strike the right balance between formality and friendliness, ensuring your message is clear and compelling. With ChatGPT, you can compose an email requesting a meeting, with the AI suggesting phrasing that captures both your intent and your tone. It might structure the email with a polite greeting, clearly state the purpose, and end with a courteous sign-off. This not only saves time but ensures your communication remains professional and effective. On a lighter note, suppose you're planning a weekend get-together and want to invite friends. ChatGPT can help craft a friendly email, suggesting language that feels warm and inviting. Tailoring the message to fit the occasion ensures you convey enthusiasm and hospitality, setting the tone for a joyful gathering.

Beyond emails, text messaging is another area where ChatGPT shines. Picture this: you need to reschedule an appointment, and clarity is paramount to avoid misunderstandings. ChatGPT can draft a concise message that communicates your need to change the date while expressing appreciation for the recipient's flexibility. By choosing words carefully, it helps maintain a positive rapport. Similarly, when you want to express gratitude for a thoughtful gift, ChatGPT assists in writing a thank-you message that feels genuine and heartfelt. It can suggest including specific details about why the gift was meaningful, adding a personal touch that enhances the recipient's appreciation. These examples illustrate how ChatGPT streamlines communication and enriches the personal connections we nurture through our words.

Social media is a vibrant space where engaging content reigns supreme. Crafting posts that capture attention and convey your message can be challenging, yet ChatGPT simplifies this process. Suppose you've landed a new job and want to share the news on Facebook. ChatGPT can draft a post that highlights your excitement and gratitude, encouraging your network to celebrate with you. It might suggest a blend of professional achievements and personal reflections, creating a well-rounded announcement. For visual platforms like Instagram, where captions complement images, ChatGPT helps generate catchy captions that resonate with your audience. If you're sharing a vacation photo, it can propose a caption that captures the essence of your experience, drawing viewers into your adventure. This versatility ensures that no matter the platform, your social media presence remains engaging and authentic.

In conversations, whether at networking events or family gatherings, having a few conversation starters up your sleeve can make all the difference. ChatGPT can suggest topics that help break the ice, fostering meaningful interactions. For a business networking event, ask about recent industry trends or seek advice on professional growth, sparking insightful discussions. At a family dinner, it could suggest discussing a recent travel experience or a shared hobby, creating moments of connection and laughter. By providing these conversation starters, ChatGPT equips you to navigate social settings with confidence, ensuring that you leave a lasting impression. This ability to facilitate engaging dialogue extends beyond formal scenarios, enriching everyday interactions with those around you.

3.3 CHATGPT FOR EDUCATIONAL PURPOSES

Imagine sitting at your desk, a daunting pile of homework staring back at you. The clock ticks, and your patience wears thin. This is where ChatGPT steps in, transforming your study sessions into streamlined experiences. Let's start with homework help. When you're grappling with complex concepts, like the principles of photosynthesis, ChatGPT becomes your personal tutor. You can ask it to break down these scientific processes into digestible bits, making it easier to grasp the core ideas. Need help with math? You may be stuck on calculating the area of a circle with a radius of 5 cm. Simply input your query, and ChatGPT will guide you through the formula, providing the answer and the steps involved in solving the problem. This interactive assistance can demystify challenging topics, helping you build confidence in your academic abilities.

Creating study guides and summaries is another area where ChatGPT shines. Preparing for an exam on the American Revolution? ChatGPT can help you summarize key points, offering a concise overview of significant battles, political changes, and influential figures. This not only saves time but also ensures you focus on the most critical information. Similarly, if you're tackling Harper Lee's "To Kill a Mockingbird," ChatGPT can aid in creating a study guide for its first chapter. It organizes themes, character insights, and plot developments, making it easier to understand and analyze the text. This structured approach transforms how you study, allowing you to engage with material more effectively and retain information longer.

Language learning is often a daunting task, but ChatGPT makes it more accessible and enjoyable. Whether you're planning a trip or simply aiming to broaden your linguistic skills, this AI tool becomes an invaluable resource. Suppose you're curious about how to say, "Where is the nearest train station?" in Spam ChatGPT can provide an accurate translation, ensuring yc communicate effectively in a foreign language. Beyond translation, it offers lists of common phrases, such as essential French expressions for travelers. By familiarizing yourself with these phrases, you gain confidence to navigate new environments, enhancing your travel experiences and cultural interactions. This capability to learn languages on the go can be a game-changer for both casual learners and dedicated students.

Research assistance is another powerful application of ChatGPT, particularly for students and professionals conducting in-depth investigations. When tasked with a research paper on climate change, you might wonder where to start. ChatGPT can suggest credible sources and recommend databases or online journals, providing a solid foundation for your work. It can also generate outlines for projects, like a history presentation on Ancient Egypt. By proposing a structured framework, ChatGPT ensures your research is organized and comprehensive, streamlining the writing process. This guidance helps you focus on analysis and interpretation rather than getting bogged down by sourcing information. The ability to support research efforts is invaluable, enabling you to tackle complex topics with clarity and purpose.

These educational applications of ChatGPT demonstrate its versatility as a learning tool. From simplifying homework to enhancing language skills, it offers tailored support to meet diverse academic needs. Whether you're a student navigating school assignments or an adult pursuing lifelong learning, ChatGPT provides resources that empower you to achieve your educational goals with confidence and efficiency. It's more than just a digital assistant; it's a partner in your learning journey, equipped to guide you through the complexities of education with ease and reliability.

3.4 MANAGING FINANCES WITH AI ASSISTANCE

Navigating the world of personal finance can feel daunting, with numbers and decisions looming large. Yet, with ChatGPT as your digital assistant, managing your finances becomes less about stress and more about strategy. Budget planning is the cornerstone of financial stability, and ChatGPT excels in helping you create a budget that aligns with your lifestyle. Imagine you have a household income of $5,000 a month. By asking ChatGPT to "Create a monthly budget," you receive a detailed breakdown of expenses, savings, and discretionary spending. This helps in organizing your finances and highlights areas where adjustments can lead to savings. If you're looking to tighten the purse strings further, ChatGPT can suggest practical ways to cut expenses. It might propose reducing dining out, finding cheaper utility providers, or setting a cap on non-essential purchases, providing a clear path to save more each month.

Tracking expenses is another critical aspect of financial management, and ChatGPT simplifies this process. Think of it as a digital ledger, ready to log daily expenses with precision. You might ask, "Help me log today's expenses: $50 on groceries and $20 on gas." Instantly, ChatGPT records these transactions, keeping a running tally of your spending. At the end of the week, it can generate an expense report summarizing where your money went. This transparency allows you to identify spending patterns and make informed decisions. By having a clear picture of your financial habits, you gain control, enabling you to adjust and allocate your budget more effectively. This proactive approach to expense tracking ensures that you remain on top of your finances, avoiding unnecessary debt and fostering a healthier financial future.

When it comes to investments, ChatGPT acts as a knowledgeable guide, offering insights into the complex world of stocks and bonds. You might wonder about the fundamental differences between these two investment types. ChatGPT can explain that stocks represent ownership in a company, with the potential for high returns and risks, while bonds are loans to corporations or governments, offering steady income with lower risk. For beginners, ChatGPT can suggest investment strategies that align with your financial goals, such as diversifying your portfolio to minimize risk or focusing on index funds for long-term growth. It provides a foundation of understanding that empowers you to make informed investment decisions. While ChatGPT offers general advice, it's important to remember that consulting with a financial advisor is wise for personalized investment strategies.

Setting and tracking financial goals is a crucial step toward achieving long-term financial stability, and ChatGPT can play a pivotal role in this process. Consider setting a savings goal to buy a car in two years. ChatGPT can help you calculate the amount needed each month to reach this target, taking into account your current savings and potential interest earnings. By providing regular updates on your progress, ChatGPT keeps you motivated and focused. Similarly, if you're planning for retirement, ChatGPT can assist in tracking your contributions and projecting future savings growth. This continuous monitoring ensures that you stay on track, offering peace of mind and confidence in your financial planning. With ChatGPT, setting and achieving financial goals becomes a structured and attainable endeavor, transforming aspirations into reality.

Incorporating ChatGPT into your financial routine offers a strategic advantage, turning complex tasks into manageable actions. Whether you're budgeting, tracking expenses, seeking investment advice, or setting financial goals, ChatGPT provides the tools and insights needed to navigate your financial landscape with confidence and clarity. As you engage with this AI assistant, you discover a newfound ease in managing your finances, empowering you to make informed decisions and build a secure financial future. Through its capabilities, ChatGPT not only simplifies financial management but also enhances your understanding, equipping you with the knowledge to thrive financially.

3.5 CHATGPT IN HEALTH AND WELLNESS

Incorporating fitness into your routine can be daunting, especially if you need help figuring out where to start. Here, ChatGPT becomes your virtual personal trainer, tailoring workout plans to fit your needs. Suppose you ask it to "Create a weekly workout plan for a beginner." ChatGPT can suggest a balanced regimen that includes cardio, strength training, and flexibility exercises, ensuring a comprehensive approach to fitness. If you're interested in improving cardiovascular health, you might inquire, "Suggest exercises for improving cardiovascular health." ChatGPT could recommend activities like brisk walking, cycling, or interval training, each designed to elevate your heart rate and boost endurance. By providing structured guidance, ChatGPT helps you embark on a fitness path that aligns with your goals, making exercise an achievable and enjoyable part of your life.

Diet and nutrition often seem complex, with countless advice and diet trends vying for attention. ChatGPT simplifies this by offering personalized meal-planning assistance. If you're exploring plant-based eating, you could ask, "Generate a meal plan for a vegetarian diet." The AI might suggest a variety of dishes rich in protein and nutrients, from lentil soups to quinoa salads, ensuring you receive a balanced intake of essential vitamins and minerals. Curious about the benefits of a balanced diet? Ask ChatGPT to "Explain the benefits of a balanced diet," and it will outline how diverse nutrients support bodily functions, improve energy levels, and enhance overall health. By demystifying nutrition, ChatGPT empowers you to make informed dietary choices that promote well-being.

Mental health is just as crucial as physical health, and ChatGPT offers valuable insights into maintaining a healthy mind. Managing stress is a common challenge, and you might seek advice by asking, "Suggest relaxation techniques for reducing stress." ChatGPT can provide a range of options, from mindfulness meditation to progressive muscle relaxation, helping you identify methods that resonate with you. Improving sleep quality is another area where ChatGPT can assist. You could inquire, "Provide tips for improving sleep quality," and receive suggestions like establishing a bedtime routine, minimizing screen time before bed, and creating a calming sleep environment. These strategies not only enhance your sleep but also contribute to better mental resilience and emotional balance, fostering mental clarity and peace of mind.

Monitoring health metrics is integral to understanding your wellness journey, and ChatGPT simplifies this process. Imagine wanting to track your hydration levels; you might ask, "Log my daily water intake." ChatGPT can assist in setting reminders and keeping a record of your consumption, ensuring you meet your hydration goals. Similarly, if you're participating in a fitness challenge, you could request, "Track my progress in a 30-day fitness challenge." ChatGPT can help chart your workouts, note improvements in strength or endurance, and keep you motivated to reach your objectives. By providing a clear picture of your health metrics, ChatGPT supports your commitment to wellness, helping you stay accountable and motivated on your health journey.

3.6 LEVERAGING CHATGPT FOR HOME AUTOMATION

Imagine stepping into a home where everything works in harmony with your needs. ChatGPT makes this vision a reality through its seamless integration with smart home devices. It's like having a conductor orchestrating your daily routines with precision. Picture this: you wake up to a gentle glow from your smart lights, perfectly timed to ease you into the day. ChatGPT has set them to turn on just as your coffee maker begins brewing that perfect cup. Such synchronization transforms mornings into a symphony of efficiency. Beyond just lights and coffee, ChatGPT can manage your thermostats and security systems too. Imagine controlling these with simple voice commands, adjusting the temperature, or checking the security status without lifting a finger. It adapts to your preferences, ensuring comfort and safety are always at your fingertips.

Managing daily tasks efficiently is crucial, and ChatGPT excels in setting automated reminders. Consider this scenario: it's easy to forget mundane but necessary tasks like taking out the trash. With ChatGPT, you can set a reminder every Monday evening to ensure you never miss waste collection day. Similarly, it can remind you to water your plants every three days, keeping your greenery thriving with minimal effort. These reminders, though simple, free up your mental space for more important decisions, reducing the cognitive load of remembering trivial tasks. This level of automation keeps your household running smoothly and liberates you from the cycle of constant reminders, letting technology shoulder the burden of routine.

Household management often feels like juggling multiple responsibilities. ChatGPT helps balance these tasks effortlessly. Consider the weekly chore of cleaning. You can instruct ChatGPT to generate a cleaning schedule, breaking tasks into manageable weekly segments. It could suggest vacuuming on Mondays, dusting on Wednesdays, and mopping on Fridays, ensuring your home remains tidy without overwhelming your schedule. Similarly, when planning meals for the week, ChatGPT can create a grocery list based on your meal plans. This organization streamlines shopping, ensuring you have everything you need while minimizing waste. By taking charge of these logistical tasks, ChatGPT transforms household management from a chaotic endeavor into a structured routine.

Entertainment is the spice of life, and ChatGPT enhances this aspect by personalizing your leisure activities. Imagine settling in for a movie night but unsure of what to watch. ChatGPT can suggest movies or TV shows tailored to your preferences, considering past likes and current mood. It might recommend a gripping thriller if you're in the mood for excitement, or a heartwarming comedy for a light-hearted evening. Beyond just recommendations, ChatGPT can craft playlists for any occasion. Whether you're hosting a dinner party or unwinding after a long day, it curates music that sets the right tone, enriching your experience. This personalized touch transforms ordinary moments into memorable ones, making entertainment effortlessly enjoyable.

Textual Element: Smart Home Setup Checklist

- **Morning Routine**: Automate smart lights and coffee makers.
- **Voice Commands**: Control thermostats and security systems.
- **Automated Reminders**: Set reminders for trash collection and plant watering.
- **Cleaning Schedule**: Organize weekly chores into a manageable plan.

- **Grocery List**: Generate based on meal plans for efficient shopping.
- **Entertainment**: Get personalized movie and music recommendations.

ChatGPT's role in home automation extends beyond simple commands; it integrates into your lifestyle, enhancing comfort and efficiency. By taking charge of routine tasks and personalizing your environment, you are free to focus on what truly matters. With technology handling the details, you can enjoy a home that adapts to your needs, ensuring every day runs smoothly and with less effort. This chapter has explored the ways ChatGPT can revolutionize your living space, making it smarter and more responsive. As we move forward, we'll delve into how these innovations impact professional settings, transforming the way we work and collaborate.

CHAPTER 4
PROFESSIONAL USE CASES

Picture a bustling marketing department, where ideas flow as freely as the coffee, and every team member is constantly on the lookout for that next big campaign. In the heart of this creative chaos, ChatGPT emerges as a digital ally, ready to revolutionize how marketing professionals brainstorm, personalize content, and stay ahead of industry trends. You might be a seasoned marketer or a novice just entering the field. Either way, understanding how to leverage AI like ChatGPT can elevate your approach, making your campaigns not only more effective but also more innovative.

Let's consider the challenge of creating engaging campaigns. The pressure to captivate audiences is immense, especially when targeting savvy groups like millennials. Here, ChatGPT steps in as a brainstorming partner, generating fresh ideas for social media campaigns that resonate with this demographic. Imagine being stuck in a creative rut, and with a simple command, ChatGPT offers a range of innovative strategies—from interactive polls to influencer partnerships—that align with millennial interests. It doesn't stop at brainstorming. When launching a new product, ChatGPT can assist in drafting a press release that captures attention, ensuring your message is clear, concise, and compelling. By integrating AI into the creative process, you open the door to new possibilities, turning potential roadblocks into stepping stones for success.

Personalization is the cornerstone of effective marketing, and ChatGPT excels in tailoring content to fit diverse audience segments. Consider the challenge of crafting personalized email templates for various customer personas. Each persona has unique needs and preferences, and ChatGPT helps you navigate this complexity by generating emails that speak directly to those differences. Whether addressing a young professional seeking career advice or a retiree exploring travel options, the AI ensures that each message feels personal and relevant. Similarly, when writing targeted ad copy, ChatGPT adjusts the language and tone to appeal to specific demographics, enhancing engagement and conversion rates. This level of customization not only streamlines your marketing efforts but also builds stronger connections with your audience, fostering brand loyalty and trust.

In the digital age, mastering search engine optimization (SEO) is crucial for ensuring your content reaches its intended audience. ChatGPT offers invaluable assistance in this area, helping you optimize your content for search engines. Imagine needing to generate a list of relevant keywords for a blog post on digital marketing. ChatGPT swiftly analyzes current trends and suggests keywords that boost visibility and drive traffic. Additionally, when crafting meta descriptions for your website pages, ChatGPT provides concise summaries that encapsulate the essence of your content while enticing potential visitors. This strategic use of AI in SEO enhances your online presence and ensures your content stands out in a crowded digital landscape, making it easier for people to discover what you have to offer.

Understanding and analyzing marketing trends is another area where ChatGPT proves invaluable. As the digital landscape evolves, staying informed about the latest trends is essential for maintaining a competitive edge. ChatGPT can summarize the latest developments in influencer marketing, providing insights into emerging platforms and strategies that are shaping the industry. ChatGPT helps you adapt your strategies to maximize reach and effectiveness by analyzing social media algorithms' impact on engagement rates. Whether you're exploring new trends or evaluating existing ones, ChatGPT serves as a critical tool for making informed decisions, ensuring that your marketing efforts remain relevant and impactful.

Interactive Element: Marketing Strategy Brainstorming

- **Campaign Ideas**: Use ChatGPT to generate fresh concepts for social media campaigns that target specific demographics.
- **Press Release Drafting**: Utilize ChatGPT to craft clear and engaging press releases for product launches.
- **Email Personalization**: Guide ChatGPT in creating personalized email templates for different customer personas.
- **SEO Optimization**: Leverage ChatGPT to suggest keywords and meta descriptions that enhance search visibility.
- **Trend Analysis**: Ask ChatGPT to summarize and analyze current marketing trends to inform your strategies.

Incorporating ChatGPT into your marketing toolkit transforms how you approach challenges, providing innovative solutions that enhance creativity, personalization, and strategic planning. As you explore these applications, you'll discover new ways to connect with your audience and elevate your marketing efforts, positioning yourself at the forefront of industry innovation.

4.1 STREAMLINING CUSTOMER SERVICE WITH CHATGPT

Imagine stepping into a bustling customer service center, where voices blend into a cacophony of inquiries and resolutions. Here, efficiency is key, and ChatGPT emerges as a powerful ally in streamlining operations. Automated response systems powered by ChatGPT can transform how you handle customer interactions. Picture drafting responses to common inquiries—those repetitive questions that flood your inbox daily. Whether it's a query about shipping times or return policies, ChatGPT crafts precise and polite replies, ensuring consistency and saving precious time. But it doesn't stop there. When faced with frequently reported issues, ChatGPT assists in generating comprehensive troubleshooting guides. These guides empower customers to resolve problems independently, reducing the load on service agents and enhancing customer satisfaction. This automation not only boosts efficiency but also ensures your team can focus on more complex, high-value interactions.

Personalization in customer service is more than a nicety; it's a necessity. ChatGPT excels in enhancing interactions by tailoring responses to individual customers. Imagine greeting each customer with a personalized message, acknowledging their unique history with your business. ChatGPT can craft these greetings, making each interaction feel special and valued. It analyzes customer purchase history to tailor responses, offering relevant solutions or upsell opportunities. For instance, if a customer frequently buys a specific product, ChatGPT suggests complementary items, creating a personalized shopping experience. This level of customization fosters loyalty, as customers appreciate the attention to detail and feel more connected to your brand. By leveraging ChatGPT, you transform generic interactions into personalized experiences, building stronger relationships with each customer.

Round-the-clock availability is a game-changer in customer service. ChatGPT enables you to provide 24/7 support, ensuring no inquiry goes unanswered, regardless of the hour. Setting up an AI chatbot to handle after-hours inquiries means customers receive immediate assistance, even when your team is offline. This chatbot can manage various requests, from FAQs to product information, ensuring customers find the answers they seek. For common support tickets, ChatGPT drafts thoughtful responses, maintaining a consistent and helpful tone. This seamless support system assures customers that help is always available, enhancing trust and satisfaction. In a world where instant gratification is expected, offering continuous support sets your service apart, demonstrating your commitment to customer care.

Understanding customer feedback is critical for continuous improvement, and ChatGPT plays a pivotal role in this analysis. Imagine sifting through mountains of surveys and reviews, where valuable insights lie hidden in plain sight. ChatGPT summarizes this feedback efficiently, highlighting key themes and concerns. It identifies areas where customers are delighted and pinpoint issues needing attention. From this analysis, ChatGPT generates action plans, offering strategic recommendations for enhancement. Whether it's improving a product feature or refining service processes, these insights guide informed decisions, driving your business forward. This capability ensures you remain attuned to customer needs, adapting and evolving in response to their feedback.

By integrating ChatGPT into your customer service operations, you unlock a new level of efficiency and personalization. It empowers you to handle inquiries swiftly, tailor interactions to individual customers, and provide unwavering support around the clock. Additionally, you gain valuable insights that inform strategic improvements by analyzing customer feedback. As you embrace these innovations, your customer service evolves, meeting the demands of modern consumers with agility and foresight.

4.2 USING CHATGPT IN CONTENT CREATION

Imagine the challenge of consistently producing high-quality content in a digital age where attention spans are fleeting and competition is fierce. ChatGPT stands as a remarkable ally for content creators, offering a wealth of tools to streamline and enhance the creation process. Whether you're drafting blog posts or crafting engaging social media content, this AI can be your creative partner. When tackling blog writing, for instance, ChatGPT assists in structuring ideas into coherent outlines. Suppose you're working on a blog post about remote work productivity. ChatGPT can help design an outline highlighting key points such as time management, workspace organization, and work-life balance. This structured approach not only organizes your thoughts but also ensures a logical flow that captivates readers.

Beyond outlines, crafting the opening lines of an article often sets the tone for the entire piece. Let's say you're tasked with writing about sustainable living. ChatGPT can draft the first paragraph, introducing the topic with clarity and intrigue and setting the stage for a compelling narrative that draws readers in. Imagine the potential: you input a few key themes, and ChatGPT generates a polished introduction that captures the essence of the topic. This capability saves time and sparks inspiration, allowing you to focus on refining and expanding upon the content.

The realm of social media demands concise yet impactful communication. Here, ChatGPT excels at generating engaging posts that resonate with audiences across platforms. Consider the challenge of composing a Twitter thread on the benefits of AI in business. ChatGPT can suggest succinct points, each building upon the last, to create a cohesive narrative. This ability to distill complex ideas into bite-sized insights makes your message accessible and engaging, ensuring it stands out in a crowded feed. Similarly, when crafting Instagram captions for a travel brand, ChatGPT offers creative suggestions that capture the spirit of adventure and allure, enticing followers to explore further.

Video content is another area where ChatGPT proves invaluable. Writing scripts for videos requires a balance of information and entertainment, a task ChatGPT handles with finesse. Suppose you're creating a YouTube tutorial on using ChatGPT itself. The AI can draft a script that guides viewers step-by-step, explaining features and functionalities in an approachable manner. It ensures clarity and coherence, maintaining viewer engagement throughout the video. Additionally, when introducing a company in a promotional video, ChatGPT can craft an introduction that highlights core values and unique selling points, setting the tone for a persuasive and memorable presentation.

Content creation doesn't end with the initial draft. Editing and proofreading are critical to ensuring clarity and coherence, tasks where ChatGPT offers support. Imagine finalizing a blog post, and you're wondering if the grammar is spot-on or if the flow is just right. ChatGPT can proofread the text, identify grammatical errors, and suggest improvements that enhance readability. It acts as a second set of eyes, meticulously reviewing content to ensure it aligns with your voice and message. This support not only elevates the quality of your writing but also boosts confidence, knowing your content is polished and professional.

With ChatGPT as your creative partner, content creation transforms from a solitary endeavor into a collaborative process. Its capabilities streamline drafting, enhance creativity, and ensure precision, allowing you to focus on what matters most—delivering valuable and engaging content to your audience. Whether you're a seasoned writer or a novice exploring new territories, ChatGPT offers a versatile and dynamic toolset that adapts to your needs, empowering you to elevate your content creation efforts to new heights.

4.3 CHATGPT FOR MARKET RESEARCH AND ANALYSIS

In the fast-paced world of business, staying ahead of the competition requires a keen understanding of the market landscape. ChatGPT proves to be an invaluable tool in conducting competitor analysis. Picture yourself tasked with generating a competitor analysis report for the tech industry. This is where ChatGPT's ability to process vast amounts of data becomes crucial. It can sift through news articles, industry reports, and social media mentions to compile a detailed overview of your competitors. By summarizing the strengths and weaknesses of a competing brand, ChatGPT helps you identify areas where your business can differentiate itself. It might highlight a competitor's strong customer service reputation but also point out their less robust product range. Such insights allow you to strategize effectively, capitalizing on opportunities they might have overlooked.

Keeping a pulse on market trends is equally vital for making informed business decisions. ChatGPT excels in identifying and summarizing these trends. Imagine you're exploring the renewable energy sector, a rapidly evolving field with a plethora of factors at play. ChatGPT can analyze current articles, research papers, and industry forecasts to provide a comprehensive view of the landscape. It identifies emerging technologies, regulatory changes, and shifts in consumer preferences, helping you navigate this complex environment with confidence. Similarly, understanding consumer behavior trends is crucial for tailoring products and services to meet market demands. ChatGPT highlights patterns in purchasing habits, preferences, and emerging interests, offering a clearer picture of where the market is heading. Armed with this information, you can align your strategies to meet these evolving needs, ensuring your business remains relevant and competitive.

Surveys are a powerful tool for gathering direct feedback from consumers, yet crafting effective questions and analyzing responses can be daunting. ChatGPT simplifies this process by assisting in survey creation and analysis. Suppose you're developing a customer satisfaction survey. ChatGPT can suggest precise questions that target key areas of interest, ensuring you gather actionable insights. Questions range from rating product satisfaction to suggestions for improvement, each crafted to elicit valuable feedback. Once the survey responses are in, ChatGPT helps analyze the data, generating a summary report that highlights trends and areas of concern. It might reveal that customers love the product quality but find delivery times lacking. This analysis guides your next steps, enabling you to address issues and capitalize on strengths. By streamlining this process, ChatGPT allows you to focus on implementing changes that enhance customer satisfaction and loyalty.

Industry reports serve as a cornerstone for strategic planning, providing a deep dive into sector-specific trends and forecasts. ChatGPT can generate these reports with remarkable efficiency.

Imagine needing an industry report on the future of e-commerce. ChatGPT collects data from various sources, including economic forecasts, technological advancements, and consumer behavior analysis, compiling them into a cohesive document. It outlines potential growth areas, challenges, and innovations shaping the industry. Furthermore, ChatGPT can summarize key insights from recent market studies, distilling complex data into understandable and actionable information. This ability to synthesize vast amounts of information into concise, readable reports empowers you to make informed decisions, ensuring you stay ahead in your industry. With ChatGPT handling the bulk of the analysis, you can focus on strategic planning and execution, leveraging insights to drive your business forward.

4.4 ENHANCING TEAM COLLABORATION WITH AI

Imagine stepping into a bustling office where teamwork is key to success. Here, ChatGPT shines as a tool that streamlines collaboration, making it easier to keep everyone on the same page. One of its standout features is generating concise summaries of team meetings. After a project kickoff meeting, for instance, ChatGPT can sift through notes and discussions to highlight key points. It organizes these insights into a clear and concise summary, ensuring that everyone knows the project's goals and initial decisions. This clarity reduces misunderstandings and keeps the team focused on shared objectives. Similarly, after a brainstorming session, ChatGPT can draft follow-up action items. It captures the creative energy of the meeting and translates it into actionable steps, ensuring ideas don't get lost once the session ends.

Collaborative document creation is another area where ChatGPT proves invaluable. In projects that require input from multiple team members, it acts as a facilitator. Imagine working on a project proposal. ChatGPT helps integrate contributions from various colleagues into a cohesive document, keeping the language consistent and the arguments aligned. This not only saves time but also enhances the quality of the final proposal. When preparing a report on quarterly performance, ChatGPT assists by compiling data and insights from different departments. It ensures that the report reflects a unified perspective, presenting the company's achievements and areas for improvement in a clear and engaging manner. By streamlining the drafting process, ChatGPT frees team members to focus on analysis and strategy rather than getting bogged down in document logistics.

Internal communication is the lifeblood of any organization, and ChatGPT significantly enhances this by automating routine messages. Suppose it's time to draft weekly team updates and announcements. ChatGPT can craft these messages with a tone that aligns with corporate culture, ensuring they are informative and engaging. It might include highlights of the week, upcoming deadlines, and motivational quotes to keep morale high. In a similar vein, ChatGPT helps create templates for internal memos and notices. Whether it's a policy change or a reminder about an upcoming event, the AI ensures that the message is clear, concise, and consistent with organizational standards. This automation reduces the time spent on repetitive tasks, allowing team members to concentrate on more strategic initiatives.

When it comes to task delegation and tracking, ChatGPT serves as a reliable assistant. Imagine assigning tasks based on team member strengths. ChatGPT can analyze skills and past performance to recommend who might be best suited for each responsibility. This ensures tasks are allocated efficiently, maximizing productivity and job satisfaction. Additionally, ChatGPT generates progress reports on ongoing projects, offering a snapshot of where things stand. It highlights completed tasks, pending items, and potential roadblocks, providing managers with the insights needed to make informed decisions. These reports are invaluable for keeping projects on track, ensuring that deadlines are met and objectives achieved. By handling these logistical elements, ChatGPT lets team leaders focus on motivating and guiding their teams rather than getting lost in day-to-day minutiae.

4.5 CHATGPT IN PROJECT MANAGEMENT

Imagine standing at the helm of a project with a multitude of tasks demanding your attention. Project management is the art of juggling these responsibilities efficiently, and ChatGPT steps in as an adept assistant, easing the burden of planning and execution. When creating a detailed project plan, ChatGPT can assist in drafting a comprehensive timeline. It outlines key milestones and deadlines, ensuring that every phase of the project is accounted for. This clarity helps visualize the project from inception to completion, making it easier to anticipate potential bottlenecks. Additionally, ChatGPT can generate a risk assessment report for new projects. It identifies possible challenges, evaluates their impact, and suggests mitigation strategies. This proactive approach equips you with the foresight needed to navigate uncertainties, enhancing your ability to steer the project toward success.

Resource allocation is another critical aspect of project management where ChatGPT proves invaluable. Imagine planning a marketing campaign with resources scattered across teams and departments. ChatGPT can help you create a resource allocation plan, detailing how personnel, time, and budget will be distributed. It ensures that each aspect of the campaign has the necessary support, optimizing efficiency and effectiveness. Furthermore, when drafting a budget proposal for project resources, ChatGPT can assist in itemizing costs, evaluating financial constraints, and proposing adjustments. This meticulous approach not only streamlines budgeting but also ensures that financial resources are aligned with project goals. By leveraging ChatGPT for resource allocation, you transform a complex task into a manageable process, facilitating smoother project execution.

Once a project is underway, tracking progress becomes paramount. ChatGPT excels in monitoring and reporting on project milestones. It can generate weekly project status updates, providing a snapshot of where things stand. These updates highlight completed tasks, pending actions, and any deviations from the plan, offering invaluable insights for decision-making. Additionally, ChatGPT can summarize project deliverables and completion rates, ensuring stakeholders are informed of achievements and progress. This transparency fosters accountability and keeps the project aligned with its objectives. By effectively tracking progress, you can make informed adjustments, ensuring the project remains on track and within scope.

Effective communication with stakeholders is vital to project success, and ChatGPT enhances this by streamlining interactions. Imagine needing to update stakeholders on project developments. ChatGPT can draft project update emails, articulating key achievements and upcoming goals. These communications are clear, concise, and tailored to the audience, ensuring stakeholders remain engaged and informed. Additionally, ChatGPT can assist in creating presentations that summarize project achievements, offering a visual and compelling overview of progress. This enhances stakeholder understanding and reinforces confidence in your management capabilities. By utilizing ChatGPT for stakeholder communication, you ensure that all parties are aligned with the project's vision and trajectory, fostering a collaborative and supportive environment.

Through these applications, ChatGPT becomes an indispensable tool in project management. It aids in planning, resource allocation, progress monitoring, and stakeholder communication, transforming how projects are executed and managed. As you integrate ChatGPT into your project management processes, you unlock efficiencies and insights that enhance your ability to deliver successful outcomes. This chapter has explored the multifaceted role ChatGPT plays in professional settings, and as we continue, we'll delve into the creative and artistic realms, where AI opens new horizons for innovation and expression.

SHARE THE MAGIC OF LEARNING

"The greatest joy in life comes from helping others find their way."

ALBERT SCHWEITZER

Thank you for picking up *Master ChatGPT Effortlessly!* If you've enjoyed learning how to make ChatGPT work for you, would you consider helping others on this journey?

Your review can be the guide someone else needs to decide if *Master ChatGPT Effortlessly* is right for them. People often choose books based on reviews, and by leaving yours, you're helping one more reader unlock the amazing things ChatGPT can do.

Writing a review is easy and quick—it only takes a minute, but the impact lasts. Your words might help...

- one more student understand tech tools better,
- one more writer create a story,
- one more friend discover the joy of using ChatGPT,
- one more person find the confidence to try something new.

If you'd like to make a difference, simply scan the QR code below and leave your review:

Thank you from the bottom of my heart for being a part of this mission. Together, we're helping others explore, create, and learn with ChatGPT!

Samuel Thorpe

CHAPTER 5
CREATIVE AND ARTISTIC APPLICATIONS

I magine unlocking a hidden world where words dance on the page, each sentence a brushstroke painting vivid scenes in the mind's eye. This is the realm of creative writing, where stories and poetry breathe life into our imaginations. ChatGPT is your guide, ready to transform your creative ideas into structured narratives and evocative verse. Whether you're crafting the next great mystery novel or composing a haiku that captures the essence of a fleeting moment, this tool bridges the gap between inspiration and creation, offering support and guidance at every step.

5.1 WRITING STORIES AND POETRY WITH CHATGPT

Creating a compelling story often begins with an outline, a structured map that guides your narrative journey. ChatGPT excels in helping you develop detailed story outlines, providing a framework to flesh out ideas into a coherent plot. Imagine you're setting your story in a quaint, mysterious small town. You might prompt ChatGPT to "Generate a plot outline for a mystery novel set in a small town." The AI can suggest a series of intriguing events, such as a mysterious disappearance or a hidden secret waiting to be uncovered, setting the stage for suspense and intrigue. Alongside plot development, character profiles breathe life into your story. You can request to "Create character profiles for the main protagonist and antagonist," and ChatGPT will help you flesh out their backgrounds, motivations, and conflicts. This foundation not only aids in storytelling but also ensures your characters resonate with readers, drawing them into the narrative world you've crafted.

Dialogue is the heartbeat of any story, capturing the essence of characters and driving the plot forward. Crafting realistic and engaging dialogue can be a challenging task, yet ChatGPT offers a helping hand. Consider a scene where tensions run high, like a heated argument between two characters. By instructing ChatGPT to "Write a dialogue exchange between two characters in a heated argument," you receive a vivid conversation that captures the emotional intensity of the moment. Alternatively, for a more nurturing interaction, you might ask for "Generate a conversation between a mentor and their mentee." Here, ChatGPT can craft a dialogue that conveys wisdom, encouragement, and personal growth, bringing depth and authenticity to your characters' interactions. These examples illustrate how ChatGPT serves as a dialogue coach, helping you refine the nuance and tone of your characters' voices.

Poetry is the art of distilling emotions and ideas into rhythm and meter, creating verses that resonate with readers on a profound level. ChatGPT's capabilities extend to poetry generation, offering a creative partner for exploring various poetic forms. You might be inspired to "Compose a haiku about the changing seasons." In response, ChatGPT will generate a three-line poem that captures the ephemeral beauty of nature's transitions, evoking imagery that lingers in the mind. Consider a sonnet on the theme of love for a more classical approach. By prompting ChatGPT to "Generate a sonnet on the theme of love," you'll receive a fourteen-line poem that weaves together emotion and structure, showcasing the enduring power of poetic expression. These poetic endeavors highlight ChatGPT's ability to transform abstract ideas into tangible art, enriching your creative repertoire.

In the realm of creative writing, editing, and refinement are crucial steps in polishing your work. ChatGPT offers valuable insights for enhancing your writing, acting as an editor who provides constructive feedback. Suppose you need help with the opening paragraph of a short story. You could ask ChatGPT to "Suggest improvements for a short story's opening paragraph." The AI can offer suggestions to enhance clarity, create intrigue, or refine your narrative voice. Similarly, when working on a poem, you might seek advice on the rhythm and flow. By requesting ChatGPT to "Provide feedback on the rhythm and flow of a poem," you'll receive tailored guidance to ensure your verses achieve the desired impact. This collaborative editing process empowers you to elevate your writing, transforming drafts into polished pieces that captivate and inspire.

Interactive Element: Creative Writing Exercise

- **Prompt for Plot Development**: Write a brief outline for a story set in your favorite location. Include a protagonist, an antagonist, and at least three key events.
- **Dialogue Practice**: Create a dialogue exchange between two characters experiencing a misunderstanding. Focus on how they resolve the conflict.
- **Poetry Exploration**: Compose a four-line stanza about a cherished memory. Experiment with different poetic forms and styles.

In leveraging ChatGPT's creative writing capabilities, you open doors to new possibilities, where your stories and poems flourish, guided by an AI that understands and enhances your artistic vision.

5.2 GENERATING VISUAL ART PROMPTS

Visual art is a language of its own, speaking through colors, shapes, and forms. If you're looking to fuel your creativity, ChatGPT can generate prompts that inspire drawing and sketching. Imagine being tasked with creating a futuristic cityscape, a scene that captures the awe of advanced architecture and vibrant urban life. ChatGPT might suggest envisioning towering skyscrapers with neon lights, hovering vehicles zipping between them, and bustling streets filled with diverse characters from all walks of life. Such a prompt can ignite your imagination, encouraging you to explore new techniques and perspectives in your art. Similarly, if you're venturing into character design for a fantasy novel, ChatGPT can provide prompts that challenge you to explore unique traits and qualities. You might find yourself sketching a character with ethereal wings, a mysterious aura, or a mischievous glint in their eye, each detail adding depth to their persona and enriching your visual narrative.

When it comes to brainstorming concepts for visual art projects, ChatGPT becomes an invaluable partner. Consider the possibilities for a series of paintings based on the four elements—earth, water, air, and fire. ChatGPT can help you explore how each element might be depicted, suggesting motifs, colors, and compositions that embody their essence. You might paint swirling water currents, fiery explosions, serene landscapes, or ethereal skies, each canvas capturing the unique qualities of its element. For a sci-fi themed digital art piece, ChatGPT can generate ideas that push the boundaries of imagination. Picture a world where technology and nature coexist, with cyborg creatures roaming lush landscapes or futuristic cities built within towering trees. These concepts encourage experimenting with new styles and themes, broadening your artistic horizons.

Art challenges and exercises are crucial for honing your skills, and ChatGPT has the tools to keep you motivated. Imagine embarking on a 30-day drawing challenge, each day presenting a new prompt to stretch your artistic muscles. ChatGPT could suggest themes like "draw a mythical creature" or "create a portrait using only geometric shapes," pushing you to explore different techniques and subjects. If you're focused on improving specific skills like shading and perspective, ChatGPT can recommend targeted exercises. You might practice rendering light and shadow on spherical objects or sketching urban scenes to perfect your understanding of depth and dimension. These challenges foster growth, providing the structure and inspiration needed to take your art to the next level.

Collaboration in art can lead to unexpected creativity, and ChatGPT facilitates this process easily. When generating themes for a collaborative mural, ChatGPT might propose ideas that resonate with shared values or community stories. Imagine creating a mural that celebrates cultural diversity, each section depicting elements of various traditions and histories. ChatGPT can offer prompts that guide participating artists in contributing their unique perspectives, ensuring a cohesive and meaningful final piece. For a group art project exploring cultural diversity, ChatGPT might suggest prompts that encourage participants to reflect on their heritage, share personal experiences, and express these through visual art. This collaborative approach enriches the creative process and fosters connection and understanding among artists.

5.3 ENHANCING ARTISTIC TECHNIQUES WITH CHATGPT

Artistic growth often hinges on learning new techniques and refining existing skills. ChatGPT is a valuable resource for artists of all levels, offering tutorials and tips that cater to your learning style. If you're new to oil painting, asking ChatGPT to "Explain the basics of oil painting for beginners" will provide you with foundational knowledge. You'll learn about essential supplies like brushes, palettes, and canvases and discover techniques such as layering and blending that define this medium. For digital artists, ChatGPT's guidance on "Mastering digital illustration" can introduce you to software tools, brush settings, and methods for creating dynamic compositions. These insights help demystify complex processes, empowering you to experiment with confidence and creativity.

Improving existing skills requires practice and dedication, and ChatGPT can suggest targeted exercises to enhance your artistic abilities. You may be looking to refine your anatomy drawing skills. By requesting "Generate practice exercises for improving anatomy drawing," you'll receive detailed suggestions like drawing skeletal structures or studying muscle groups from different angles. These exercises encourage you to observe and understand the human form more deeply, translating anatomical knowledge into more accurate and expressive art. Similarly, if you're aiming to deepen your understanding of color theory, ChatGPT can offer techniques for "Enhancing color theory knowledge." You might explore exercises like creating harmonious color palettes or experimenting with contrasting hues to evoke specific emotions. By engaging with these prompts, you cultivate a more nuanced approach to color, enriching your artistic expression.

Constructive feedback is invaluable in the artistic process, providing fresh perspectives and highlighting areas for improvement. ChatGPT can serve as an objective critic, offering suggestions on your work. Suppose you've completed a landscape painting and are seeking feedback. By asking ChatGPT to "Provide feedback on a completed landscape painting," you might receive insights on composition balance, color harmony, or how to enhance focal points. This guidance helps you refine your techniques, ensuring your work resonates with viewers. Similarly, ChatGPT's ability to "Suggest improvements for a graphic novel panel layout" can be instrumental for those working on graphic novels. It might advise on panel flow, dialogue placement, or visual pacing, helping you craft a more engaging and coherent narrative. These interactions foster a dynamic learning environment where feedback becomes a tool for continuous improvement.

Exploring different art styles broadens your creative horizons, allowing you to experiment and discover new facets of your artistic identity. ChatGPT encourages this exploration by generating prompts that challenge your stylistic boundaries. If you're intrigued by Impressionism, a prompt like "Generate prompts for creating art in the style of Impressionism" can guide you to capture fleeting moments with loose brushwork and vibrant colors. This exploration might involve painting en plein air or focusing on how light interacts with your subject. For those drawn to abstract art, ChatGPT can suggest exercises that push you beyond representational forms. Imagine experimenting with shapes, textures, and colors that convey emotions or concepts without depicting recognizable subjects. These exercises encourage you to think beyond traditional constraints, opening doors to new artistic possibilities and personal expression.

5.4 CHATGPT FOR MUSIC AND SOUND CREATION

Imagine the thrill of crafting a new song, the lyrics capturing emotions that words alone struggle to convey. ChatGPT steps in as a lyrical collaborator, ready to spark inspiration and refine your ideas. Suppose you're dreaming of a vibrant and catchy love song in the pop genre. By prompting ChatGPT to "Generate lyrics for a love song in the style of pop music," you receive verses that weave emotion with rhythm, capturing the essence of love's joys and complexities. Each line suggests imagery and feelings, offering a starting point for your creative process. Alternatively, you might seek a powerful chorus for a motivational anthem. Here, ChatGPT can craft a refrain that resonates with determination and hope. Imagine lines that uplift, urging listeners to persevere and chase their dreams. This collaborative effort with ChatGPT transforms songwriting into a dynamic and engaging experience, one where creativity flows freely and ideas come to life with each verse.

Creating music goes beyond lyrics; the composition itself sets the tone and mood of each piece. ChatGPT can provide valuable prompts that inspire the musical structure of your work. For instance, when composing a jazz piece, you might ask, "Suggest a chord progression for a jazz piece." With ChatGPT's guidance, you explore harmonies that evoke the complexity and improvisation jazz is known for, encouraging experimentation with sounds and rhythms. If classical music is your focus, imagine requesting, "Create a prompt for composing a classical piano sonata." ChatGPT might suggest a theme that intertwines elegance and sophistication, inviting you to explore variations and motifs that echo the great composers. These prompts serve as a catalyst, guiding you through the intricate process of music creation with clarity and inspiration, allowing your compositions to take shape with elegance and depth.

Sound design is an essential aspect of storytelling, whether in films, games, or multimedia projects. ChatGPT can assist in brainstorming sound design ideas, helping you craft immersive audio experiences. Consider the task of generating sound effects for a horror film. ChatGPT might suggest eerie whispers, chilling footsteps, or ambient creaks that build tension and suspense. These sounds create an atmosphere that heightens the audience's emotional response, drawing them deeper into the narrative. For a fantasy video game, you might seek ambient sounds that transport players to another world. ChatGPT can propose the gentle rustle of enchanted forests, the distant echoes of mystical creatures, or the soft hum of ancient magic. These auditory elements enhance immersion, allowing players to fully engage with the game environment. By collaborating with ChatGPT in sound design, you expand your creative toolkit, crafting audio landscapes that captivate and enthrall.

Music creation often thrives in collaborative settings, where diverse perspectives merge to create something extraordinary. ChatGPT can facilitate collaborative music projects by proposing themes and prompts that unify and inspire. Imagine embarking on a collaborative album with fellow musicians. ChatGPT might suggest a theme that explores the intersection of past and future, encouraging each artist to contribute their unique interpretation. This thematic cohesion fosters creativity, resulting in a cohesive and compelling collection of tracks. For a songwriting group, ChatGPT can generate prompts that spark new ideas and challenge each member's creativity. Consider a prompt that encourages writing from the perspective of a historical figure or exploring a specific emotion. These collaborative exercises build camaraderie and push creative boundaries, leading to innovative compositions that reflect the collective talent of the group.

Working with ChatGPT in collaborative settings enhances the creative process, fostering collaboration and innovation.

5.5 BRAINSTORMING CREATIVE IDEAS WITH AI

When you're embarking on a new creative project, the blank canvas or empty page can feel intimidating. That's where ChatGPT becomes an invaluable ally. Imagine you're conceptualizing a new graphic novel series. You might be searching for a unique angle, something that sets your work apart from the rest. By asking ChatGPT to brainstorm ideas, you'll be presented with a myriad of possibilities. It might suggest an intriguing setting like a dystopian future or a parallel universe where mythical creatures coexist with humans. It could propose a storyline involving a protagonist who grapples with their identity amidst societal upheaval. These sparks can ignite your creativity, providing a solid foundation upon which to build your narrative. Similarly, ChatGPT can help generate concepts that engage and captivate audiences if you're considering an interactive art installation. Picture an installation that responds to viewer movements, transforming shapes and colors in real time. This level of interactivity invites viewers to become part of the art, expanding the boundaries of traditional exhibition spaces.

Creative blocks are a common hurdle for artists and creators alike. When inspiration wanes, ChatGPT is there to rejuvenate your creativity. Suppose you're stuck on a project, feeling like you've exhausted every avenue. By requesting prompts to kickstart creativity, ChatGPT can introduce fresh perspectives. It might suggest exploring a different medium or incorporating an unexpected element into your work. For instance, if you're a painter, it could prompt you to integrate digital elements into your canvas, creating a hybrid piece that challenges conventional boundaries.

Alternatively, if you're a writer facing a stalled project, ChatGPT can generate alternative perspectives that breathe new life into your narrative. A shift in point of view or a change in setting might be just what you need to overcome creative inertia. These strategies not only help navigate creative blocks but also open up new pathways for exploration and discovery.

Collaborative brainstorming sessions are a dynamic way to refine ideas and foster innovation. Imagine organizing a virtual session for a film script, where participants from various backgrounds come together to share insights and suggestions. ChatGPT can facilitate this process by generating discussion topics that ignite conversation and encourage diverse viewpoints. It might propose exploring themes like resilience in the face of adversity or the impact of technology on human connection. These topics serve as a catalyst for dialogue, allowing participants to build on each other's ideas and craft a richer, more nuanced narrative. Similarly, in a creative writing workshop, ChatGPT can provide prompts that challenge attendees to think outside the box. It might suggest writing from the perspective of a seemingly inanimate object or crafting a story that unfolds in reverse chronological order. This collaborative environment fosters creativity, pushing participants to expand their creative horizons and produce work that is both innovative and engaging.

Once you've gathered your initial ideas, the process of refining and developing them begins. ChatGPT plays a crucial role in this phase, offering feedback and suggestions that elevate your concepts to new heights. Imagine you have a rough draft of a novel's plot. By asking ChatGPT to provide feedback, you gain insights into plot structure, character development, and pacing. It might suggest tightening certain chapters or expanding on subplots to enhance the narrative's depth and complexity. Similarly, if you're working on a visual art concept, ChatGPT can offer suggestions for expansion and enhancement. It might propose experimenting with scale, integrating multimedia elements, or exploring different color palettes. These insights help you refine your work, ensuring that your final product resonates with your audience and fulfills your creative vision. The collaboration with ChatGPT transforms the refinement process into an engaging and iterative journey, one where ideas are continually shaped and polished until they reach their full potential.

5.6 CHATGPT IN GAME DESIGN AND DEVELOPMENT

Creating immersive game worlds requires a blend of creativity and meticulous planning. Here, ChatGPT shines as a tool for generating captivating narratives and backstories that breathe life into virtual realms. Suppose you're developing a fantasy RPG set in a magical land. ChatGPT can assist by crafting a rich backstory that delves into the history of the land, its mystical creatures, and the ancient prophecies that drive the plot. This narrative foundation provides depth, inviting players to lose themselves in a world where every corner holds a new story. Character profiles are another essential element, and ChatGPT helps flesh out both main and supporting characters. Whether it's a valiant hero or a cunning villain, ChatGPT can outline their motivations, strengths, and flaws, ensuring they resonate with players and enhance the overall narrative.

Game mechanics and rules are the frameworks that guide player interactions and experiences. With ChatGPT, you can explore innovative mechanics that challenge and engage players. Imagine designing a strategy board game. ChatGPT might suggest mechanics like resource management, where players must balance short-term gains against long-term goals, or asymmetric gameplay, where each player has unique abilities and objectives. These mechanics add layers of strategy and replayability, keeping players invested. For a multiplayer card game, ChatGPT can generate rules that encourage cooperation and competition, such as drafting systems where players build their decks from a shared pool of cards. These elements create dynamic and evolving gameplay, fostering an environment where players must adapt and innovate to succeed.

Level design and layouts are crucial for maintaining player engagement and ensuring a cohesive gaming experience. ChatGPT can provide inspiration for designing game levels that challenge and intrigue players. When crafting a platformer level, you might explore the use of verticality and hidden paths to create a sense of exploration. ChatGPT can suggest including environmental hazards that test players' reflexes and timing, such as moving platforms and rotating obstacles. For puzzle games, ChatGPT can generate concepts that test players' logic and creativity, such as spatial puzzles that require manipulating objects to unlock new areas. These level designs challenge players and encourage them to think critically and experiment with different strategies.

Writing dialogue and scripts for games is an art form that captures the essence of storytelling and character development. ChatGPT can assist in crafting dialogue that enhances the game's narrative and immerses players in the story. Imagine a key interaction between characters where emotions run high. ChatGPT can help you write dialogue that conveys tension, betrayal, or camaraderie, adding depth to the characters and the story. For a game's cutscene, ChatGPT can generate a script that seamlessly integrates with the gameplay, using visual and audio cues to heighten the drama and convey critical plot points. This collaboration ensures that every word spoken and every scene played out contributes to the game's immersive experience, drawing players deeper into the narrative.

As we conclude this chapter, it's clear that ChatGPT offers versatile tools for game design and development. From crafting rich backstories and characters to designing engaging mechanics and levels, ChatGPT empowers creators to push the boundaries of interactive storytelling. It stands as a valuable ally in the creative process, enhancing each aspect of game development with fresh ideas and innovative solutions. As we transition to the next chapter, we'll explore how these creative applications extend beyond entertainment, shaping various industries and influencing everyday life.

CHAPTER 6
ADVANCED FEATURES AND CUSTOMIZATION

I magine opening the door to a bustling digital marketplace, where countless apps and tools chatter away in their own languages. In this vibrant ecosystem, APIs—or Application Programming Interfaces—act as translators, enabling these disparate systems to converse seamlessly. The API is your bridge to interconnectivity, and when it comes to ChatGPT, it transforms the way this AI can be woven into the fabric of your digital world. By integrating ChatGPT with other software, you unlock the potential to enhance applications with conversational intelligence, opening avenues for creativity and efficiency.

At its core, an API is a set of rules that allows different software applications to communicate with each other. Think of it as a universal language, enabling one program to request and send information to another effortlessly. In the context of ChatGPT, the API establishes a link between OpenAI's powerful language model and your chosen applications, facilitating smooth interactions that can enhance user experience. This communication is vital, allowing applications to leverage ChatGPT's capabilities, whether for generating content, answering queries, or automating responses. The benefits of using ChatGPT's API are manifold. It offers flexibility, enabling developers to tailor the AI's functionality to suit specific needs. Additionally, it provides scalability, accommodating growth as your application's demands increase. By tapping into ChatGPT's API, you gain a tool that adapts to your unique requirements, fostering innovation and efficiency.

Setting up API access might sound daunting, but breaking it down into manageable steps makes the process straightforward. To begin, you'll need to obtain an API key from OpenAI. This key serves as your access pass, granting permission to interact with ChatGPT's API. Once you have your key, configure your API settings to align with your project needs, ensuring compatibility and optimal performance. Authentication is a crucial step in verifying your identity and securing your connection to the API. This process typically involves adding your API key to your application's code, a step that safeguards your interactions and maintains system integrity. With these elements in place, you're ready to explore the possibilities that ChatGPT's API integration offers, setting the stage for dynamic interactions that elevate your application's capabilities.

Basic API operations form the backbone of your interactions with ChatGPT. At the simplest level, you send text to the API, a request that prompts ChatGPT to generate a response. This exchange is akin to sending a message and receiving a reply, a process that unfolds with remarkable speed and accuracy. Once you receive the AI's response, handling it becomes your next task. This involves parsing the data, extracting the needed information, and incorporating it into your application. Error handling and troubleshooting are essential components, ensuring that any hiccups in communication are swiftly resolved. By implementing robust error-handling mechanisms, you maintain a smooth flow of information, minimizing disruptions and optimizing performance.

Advanced API functionalities offer a deeper level of customization, enabling you to refine your interactions with ChatGPT. Running batch requests is one such feature, allowing you to send multiple queries simultaneously. This capability enhances efficiency, especially when dealing with large volumes of data or complex tasks. Effective use of rate limits is another consideration, as well as ensuring that your API interactions remain within acceptable parameters. Monitoring and logging API usage provide valuable insights, allowing you to track performance, identify trends, and make informed adjustments. These advanced functions empower you to tailor ChatGPT's capabilities to your specific needs, maximizing its potential and driving innovation.

Interactive Element: API Setup Checklist

- **Obtain API Key**: Secure your access by acquiring a key from OpenAI.
- **Configure Settings**: Align API configurations with project requirements.
- **Authenticate Requests**: Add your API key to ensure secure interactions.
- **Implement Error Handling**: Establish robust mechanisms for troubleshooting.
- **Utilize Advanced Functions**: Explore batch requests and monitor usage for efficiency.

By grasping the intricacies of ChatGPT's API integration, you open doors to enhanced functionality and creative possibilities. Each step, from understanding APIs to leveraging advanced features, equips you with the tools to transform your applications, enriching user experience and driving technological advancement.

6.1 CUSTOMIZING RESPONSES AND PERSONALIZATION

Imagine conversing with an old friend who knows exactly how you like your coffee, remembers your favorite movies, and uses just the right humor to make you laugh. That's the kind of tailored interaction you can create with ChatGPT when you customize its responses. Adjusting the tone and style is akin to fine-tuning a radio to your favorite station. Want a formal tone for business emails or a casual vibe for friendly chats? You can set these preferences, ensuring that ChatGPT speaks your language. It's about aligning the AI's voice with your expectations, creating a seamless dialogue that feels natural and intuitive. Setting response formats further refines this experience. Whether you need bullet points for clarity or a narrative style for storytelling, ChatGPT can adapt its responses to suit the context, making your interactions efficient and engaging. Including specific keywords or phrases tailors the content even more, guiding ChatGPT to focus on what's most relevant to you, ensuring the information it provides hits the mark every time.

Tokens and parameters are powerful tools that give you control over the nuances of ChatGPT's replies. Control tokens, for instance, allow you to regulate the length of responses. Whether you require a succinct answer or a detailed explanation, these tokens provide the flexibility to adjust the depth of information. Temperature settings introduce a creative twist, influencing how adventurous or conservative the responses are. A higher temperature invites more variability and creativity, which is perfect for brainstorming sessions. A lower setting yields more focused and predictable results, which is ideal when precision is paramount. The frequency penalty is another tool at your disposal, reducing repetition in outputs. This ensures that responses remain fresh and varied, enhancing the richness of interaction and keeping the conversation dynamic and engaging.

Creating user profiles adds a personalized touch, transforming ChatGPT from a generic tool into a bespoke assistant. By storing user preferences, you ensure that ChatGPT remembers your likes and dislikes, tailoring each interaction to reflect your unique personality. This might include your preferred topics, favorite authors, or specific interests, all of which help the AI craft responses that resonate with you. Utilizing context for personalized responses means ChatGPT doesn't just answer your questions —it understands the bigger picture. Whether you're planning a trip or exploring a new hobby, the AI draws on past interactions to provide insights that are contextually relevant and meaningful. Updating profiles based on user interactions keeps the AI attuned to your evolving preferences, ensuring that your experience remains fresh and aligned with your current interests.

Dynamic personalization brings a layer of sophistication to your interactions with ChatGPT, enabling real-time adjustments that enhance the user experience. Adapting responses based on conversation history allows the AI to weave past dialogues into current ones, creating a coherent and continuous narrative. This approach ensures continuity, making each interaction feel like an extension of the last. Real-time sentiment analysis takes this a step further, allowing ChatGPT to gauge your mood and adjust its tone accordingly. Whether you're seeking encouragement or a more analytical perspective, the AI can pivot its responses to match your emotional state, providing empathetic and responsive support. Contextual awareness in responses ensures that ChatGPT remains sensitive to the nuances of your queries, offering insights that are not only accurate but also aligned with the subtleties of your conversation. This level of personalization transforms ChatGPT into an intelligent companion capable of adapting to your needs with precision and empathy.

6.2 UTILIZING CHATGPT'S MEMORY CAPABILITIES

Imagine interacting with someone who remembers what you talked about yesterday, knows your preferences, and can recall details from previous conversations. This is the power of ChatGPT's memory capabilities. At its most basic, memory in AI can be divided into short-term and long-term categories. Short-term memory allows the AI to retain information from the current interaction, making it capable of maintaining context and coherence within a single session. Long-term memory, on the other hand, involves storing information across multiple interactions, enriching the AI's ability to provide personalized experiences over time. The benefits of memory in AI interactions are vast. They include tailoring responses to individual preferences, offering consistent user experiences, and anticipating needs based on past behaviors. However, limitations exist, such as the potential for outdated or irrelevant information to impact the quality of responses. Additionally, considerations around privacy and data security must be addressed to ensure users feel confident that their information is handled responsibly.

Incorporating memory into interactions with ChatGPT is like giving the AI a diary of your preferences and past exchanges. This capability allows the AI to store user preferences, enabling more personalized interactions. Imagine having a conversation about your favorite book genres, and the next time you chat, ChatGPT recalls this preference and suggests new book titles. This dynamic retrieval of stored information enhances the AI's ability to engage in meaningful dialogue, making it feel more like a conversation with a thoughtful friend rather than a machine. Customizing responses based on memory means that ChatGPT can adapt its replies to align with your interests and past interactions, creating a more engaging and relevant experience. For example, if you frequently ask about healthy recipes, the AI might prioritize nutritional content in its suggestions, tailoring its responses to your lifestyle.

Consider the practical applications of memory in various contexts. For customer support interactions, memory can transform how businesses engage with clients. By remembering a customer's past issues or preferences, ChatGPT can offer customized support, improving satisfaction and efficiency. In gaming applications, memory allows the AI to track a player's progress and preferences, delivering a more immersive and tailored experience. This could mean remembering a player's favorite strategies or the levels they've completed, adding depth to the gaming narrative. Education, too, benefits from memory capabilities. By tailoring educational content based on user progress, ChatGPT can offer personalized learning paths. Imagine a student using the AI to study math; the AI could retain information about the student's strengths and weaknesses, adjusting its explanations and exercises accordingly to provide targeted support.

Managing and resetting memory is crucial to maintaining the quality and relevance of interactions. Clearing memory for new interactions ensures that the previous context doesn't interfere with current conversations. This might involve resetting the AI's memory before starting a new session, allowing for fresh and unbiased interactions. Updating stored information is equally important, ensuring that the AI's memory remains accurate and reflects current preferences and needs. This might involve regularly reviewing and revising stored data to align with evolving interests or circumstances. Handling memory-related issues requires a thoughtful approach, as errors or inaccuracies in memory can impact the user experience. Implementing mechanisms to address these issues, such as allowing users to edit or delete stored information, enhances trust and ensures that the AI continues to provide valuable and relevant interactions.

6.3 ADVANCED CONFIGURATION SETTINGS

As you explore ChatGPT, you'll find a wealth of configuration options that can transform your interaction from basic to bespoke. These settings are the levers and dials you use to tune the system to your liking. At the heart of this customization lies the distinction between default and advanced settings. Default settings offer a standard experience, providing a straightforward user interface with basic functionality. It's like stepping into a familiar car, where everything is set for a typical drive. However, advanced settings allow you to dive deeper, giving you control over nuanced aspects of the system. Navigating the settings menu is your first step in this exploration. Here, you'll discover key configuration parameters that govern the behavior and performance of ChatGPT. Whether you're adjusting the verbosity of responses or altering interaction styles, these parameters provide a toolkit for tailoring your experience to align with your specific goals and preferences.

Optimizing ChatGPT's performance is akin to fine-tuning an engine for peak efficiency. It's about ensuring that the system runs smoothly, delivering responses quickly and accurately. One of the first adjustments you can make involves processing power and resources. By allocating the appropriate resources, you can enhance the system's ability to handle complex tasks without lag. Configuring response time and latency is another crucial aspect. By tweaking these settings, you can strike a balance between speed and accuracy, ensuring that ChatGPT delivers timely responses without sacrificing the quality of information. Balancing performance and cost is a consideration, especially if you're working within budget constraints. It involves making strategic decisions about resource allocation to maximize efficiency while keeping expenses in check. This configuration aspect is crucial for individuals and businesses looking to leverage ChatGPT's capabilities without breaking the bank.

Security and privacy settings are paramount in today's digital landscape, where data integrity and user confidentiality are top priorities. Within ChatGPT, data encryption settings play a critical role in safeguarding information. Encrypting data ensures that sensitive information remains protected from unauthorized access. Access controls and permissions are another layer of security, allowing you to define who can interact with the system and what level of access they have. This feature is especially important in collaborative environments, where multiple users may engage with ChatGPT. Compliance with privacy regulations is an essential consideration, particularly for businesses operating in regions with stringent data protection laws. These settings ensure that your use of ChatGPT aligns with legal requirements, providing peace of mind that your interactions adhere to best practices in data privacy.

The user interface is your primary point of contact with ChatGPT, and customizing it enhances the overall user experience. Changing themes and layouts is a simple yet effective way to personalize your interface. Whether you prefer a minimalist design or a more vibrant aesthetic, these options allow you to create a comfortable and engaging environment. Configuring notification settings is another aspect of customization, enabling you to control the flow of information and alerts. By adjusting these settings, you can ensure that you receive timely updates without being overwhelmed by unnecessary notifications. Personalizing interaction options further refines the experience. This might involve choosing how ChatGPT presents information or selecting the types of interactions that align with your needs. These customizations make the system feel more intuitive and responsive, enhancing the sense of a personalized dialogue between you and the AI.

6.4 CREATING CUSTOM CHATBOT PERSONALITIES

In the ever-evolving landscape of artificial intelligence, creating a chatbot personality is akin to giving life to a digital companion. Imagine interacting with a chatbot that not only answers your questions but does so with a flair that mirrors a favorite character or embodies the professionalism of a seasoned customer service agent. The concept of chatbot personalities is essential for crafting experiences that resonate with users, imbuing interactions with warmth, humor, or authority as needed. Custom personalities offer significant benefits. They transform generic exchanges into engaging dialogues and create a sense of familiarity and trust. By defining personality traits, you guide the chatbot's behavior, ensuring consistency in tone and style. Whether it's a friendly, conversational bot for a youth-oriented app or a formal, precise assistant for corporate environments, the possibilities are vast. Examples abound, from a witty and sarcastic chatbot that delights users with clever banter to a nurturing and supportive one that offers gentle encouragement.

Developing a detailed personality profile is the cornerstone of crafting an authentic chatbot persona. Picture it as writing a character for a novel. Begin by defining the tone and style. Is the chatbot warm and friendly, or cool and analytical? This choice will influence every interaction, setting the mood for conversations. Next, establish behavioral rules and guidelines. Consider how the chatbot responds to common queries or how it handles complex questions. These rules ensure that its behavior aligns with the defined personality, maintaining consistency across interactions. Crafting a consistent character backstory can anchor the chatbot's identity, providing context that informs its responses. This backstory need not be elaborate but should offer a framework that guides the chatbot's interactions, helping it remain true to its personality under varying circumstances.

Once the personality profile is in place, the next step is to integrate these traits into chatbot responses seamlessly. This involves using consistent language and style, as the choice of words and sentence structure should reflect the defined personality. For instance, a playful chatbot might use informal language and emojis, while a formal one sticks to precise grammar and professional wording. Incorporating personality-specific phrases further enriches the interaction. These phrases can be catchphrases or signature expressions that reinforce the chatbot's identity. Imagine a chatbot that always starts with "Howdy, partner!" for a cowboy-themed persona or "Greetings, esteemed user" for a more formal vibe. Additionally, adapting responses based on personality ensures that the chatbot remains authentic. If a user asks a difficult question, the chatbot might respond with humor if it's light-hearted or offer a detailed explanation if it's more serious.

Testing and refining chatbot personalities is an ongoing process akin to rehearsing a play until the performance is just right. User feedback sessions are invaluable in this regard. By gathering insights from real interactions, you can understand how users perceive the chatbot's personality and make necessary adjustments. Analyzing interaction logs provides a wealth of data, revealing patterns and identifying areas for improvement. Perhaps the chatbot's humor doesn't land as intended, or its formal tone feels too stiff. These insights inform iterative improvements, allowing for fine-tuning that enhances the user experience. Iterative improvement based on feedback is key. It involves making incremental changes, testing them, and refining them further. This cycle of improvement ensures that the chatbot's personality remains fresh and engaging, adapting to evolving user expectations while staying true to its core traits.

6.5 INTEGRATING CHATGPT WITH OTHER TOOLS AND PLATFORMS

In the digital age, the ability to integrate technologies across multiple platforms is a game changer. Identifying opportunities for integrating ChatGPT with other tools and platforms involves understanding common use cases and their benefits. For instance, integrating ChatGPT into a customer service platform can streamline responses, reduce wait times, and increase customer satisfaction. Similarly, incorporating ChatGPT into an e-learning platform can provide personalized tutoring, adapting to each student's learning pace and style. Successful integrations abound across industries. In e-commerce, ChatGPT can assist with user queries, provide product recommendations, and provide troubleshooting support. In healthcare, it can help patients schedule appointments or answer frequently asked questions, freeing up staff to focus on more complex tasks. The benefits of multi-platform integration extend beyond efficiency; they enhance user engagement, improve data flow, and create cohesive experiences that drive user satisfaction.

Using webhooks to connect ChatGPT with other applications opens up a world of possibilities. Webhooks are essentially automated messages sent from one app to another when something specific happens. Setting them up involves specifying a URL endpoint where events will be sent. This setup is your gateway to seamless communication between ChatGPT and other tools. Configuring webhook triggers and actions is the next step, allowing you to define what events will initiate the webhook and what actions will follow. For example, you might set a trigger for when a new customer inquiry comes in, prompting ChatGPT to generate a response. Testing and troubleshooting are crucial to ensure webhooks function as intended. This involves running tests to confirm that data is sent correctly and that the desired actions occur without errors. Mastering webhooks enables ChatGPT to interact dynamically with other systems, creating automated workflows that save time and enhance productivity.

Integrating ChatGPT with productivity tools can revolutionize how teams collaborate and manage tasks. Take Slack, for instance. By integrating ChatGPT into Slack, you can facilitate smoother communication between team members. ChatGPT can answer questions, provide updates, or even generate reports directly within a Slack channel, keeping everyone in the loop without switching applications. Trello, a popular project management tool, also benefits from ChatGPT integration. It can help prioritize tasks, suggest deadlines, and even automate routine updates, ensuring projects stay on track. When it comes to scheduling, integrating ChatGPT with Google Calendar can simplify the process of setting meetings and reminders. ChatGPT can suggest optimal times based on availability, send invites, and manage RSVPs, leaving you free to focus on the content of your meetings rather than the logistics. These integrations illustrate how ChatGPT can enhance productivity tools, turning them into more robust solutions that streamline workflows and improve efficiency.

Custom integration projects allow you to tailor ChatGPT to unique needs, creating innovative solutions that address specific challenges. Consider a customer service chatbot integrated with a CRM system. This setup allows ChatGPT to access customer data, providing personalized responses that enhance the customer experience. It can summarize email histories, analyze customer sentiment, and even suggest next steps for resolution, all while maintaining a human touch. In the realm of home automation, creating an AI-driven personal assistant with smart home integration can transform everyday living. Imagine ChatGPT managing your smart devices, adjusting lighting, controlling temperature, or even making coffee at your command. In education, developing a platform with ChatGPT-powered tutoring can offer students personalized learning experiences. The AI can adapt to each student's progress, providing tailored exercises and feedback that align with their learning pace. These custom projects showcase the versatility of ChatGPT, demonstrating how it can be molded to fit diverse applications, enhancing functionality and user engagement across sectors.

By integrating ChatGPT with other tools and platforms, you unlock its full potential, transforming it from a standalone application into a dynamic component of your digital ecosystem. This chapter has explored various integration strategies, highlighting how ChatGPT can enhance productivity, communication, and user experience. The seamless flow of information across platforms not only boosts efficiency but also enriches user interactions, paving the way for innovation and growth. As we look ahead, consider how these integrations can impact your work and personal life, opening new possibilities for collaboration and creativity.

CHAPTER 7
OVERCOMING CHALLENGES AND TROUBLESHOOTING

I magine driving a futuristic car, one that promises to take you anywhere with ease. Yet, beneath the sleek exterior, you know it's powered by a complex system that requires careful handling. Similarly, while ChatGPT offers remarkable capabilities, it also demands an understanding of its ethical and operational intricacies. As AI becomes more integrated into our daily lives, the ethical challenges it poses must not be overlooked. We are all navigating this digital landscape together, and it's crucial to address the profound implications of privacy, misinformation, and accountability.

Ethical concerns surrounding AI, including ChatGPT, are multifaceted and merit our attention. Privacy and data protection stands at the forefront, as AI systems often handle extensive volumes of personal information. This raises questions about how data is stored, used, and potentially compromised. The risk extends beyond mere data breaches; AI systems can inadvertently infer sensitive details about individuals, even from anonymized data, posing significant privacy threats (Capitol Technology University, n.d.). Another pressing issue is AI-generated misinformation. ChatGPT, while sophisticated, can occasionally produce inaccurate or misleading information, which can have real-world consequences. This underscores the importance of accountability in AI decision-making. As AI systems play larger roles in critical sectors like healthcare and finance, ensuring their accurate and responsible outputs is paramount (Simonite, 2023).

Bias in AI responses is another significant challenge, often stemming from the data used to train these systems. ChatGPT may inadvertently reflect societal biases present in its training data, leading to skewed or prejudiced outputs. For instance, if the training data overrepresents certain demographics or viewpoints, the AI might generate biased responses that perpetuate stereotypes or misinformation (Bhattacharyya, 2020). The implications are vast, affecting everything from hiring practices to content recommendations. Identifying bias requires vigilance and a deep understanding of the potential sources, such as sample bias or exclusion bias, which can skew results by underrepresenting certain groups or perspectives.

Diverse training data is crucial to mitigate bias. By ensuring datasets are representative of the real world, we can reduce skewed outcomes and foster more equitable AI interactions. Implementing fairness algorithms is another strategy designed to balance outputs and minimize prejudicial results. Regularly auditing AI outputs helps catch and correct biases, ensuring the system evolves with a fairer outlook. Involving diverse teams in AI development can further reduce bias, as varied perspectives contribute to a more comprehensive understanding of potential pitfalls (Bhattacharyya, 2020).

Promoting ethical AI usage involves several best practices. Transparent communication about AI capabilities and limitations is essential. Users must understand that while ChatGPT is a powerful tool, it is not infallible. Encouraging responsible usage means guiding users to verify AI outputs, especially concerning critical decisions. Continuous education on AI ethics is vital, preparing users to navigate the evolving landscape responsibly. As AI continues to advance, staying informed about its ethical implications ensures that technology serves human purposes without compromising our values (Simonite, 2023).

Interactive Element: Reflection Section

Consider your own interactions with AI. Reflect on moments where you encountered biased or unexpected responses. How did you address them? What steps can you take to foster more ethical AI usage in your personal and professional life? Write down your thoughts and explore ways to implement these strategies moving forward.

By understanding and addressing these ethical concerns, we can harness ChatGPT's capabilities while upholding our commitment to fairness and responsibility. The path forward requires collaboration, vigilance, and a shared dedication to using technology as a force for good.

7.1 HANDLING INACCURATE OR IRRELEVANT RESPONSES

Interacting with ChatGPT can sometimes feel like trying to have a conversation with someone who misunderstood your question. You've probably experienced this: a response that seems out of place or misses the mark entirely. This often happens when prompts are misunderstood, leading to answers that don't quite fit the bill. Misunderstandings can stem from unclear wording, lack of detail, or even when the AI doesn't interpret the context as intended. Out-of-context replies tend to occur when the AI needs help to grasp the complete picture of what you're asking, leading to responses that seem unrelated or off-target. These issues can be frustrating, but they are common hurdles in the realm of AI interactions.

Clarity in your prompts is pivotal for steering the AI in the right direction. Imagine giving directions without a map; vague prompts can leave ChatGPT wandering aimlessly. To improve the clarity of your prompts, start by providing clear and specific instructions. Rather than asking, "Tell me about apples," specify what you want to know, such as, "Explain the nutritional benefits of eating apples." This specificity narrows the AI's focus and helps it generate a response that aligns closely with your intentions. Including necessary context in your prompts is equally important. Just like a good story needs a setting, your prompts should set the scene for what you expect from the AI. For instance, if you're asking about a historical event, mentioning the time period or key figures involved can lead to a more accurate and relevant response.

Refining prompts is an iterative process, much like sculpting a piece of art. You start with a rough shape and gradually refine it until it matches your vision. Begin by evaluating the initial outputs you receive from ChatGPT. Ask yourself whether the response meets your expectations or if it seems to veer off course. If the answer is unsatisfactory, consider what might have confused the AI. Was the question too broad? Did it lack context? Once you identify these gaps, make incremental adjustments to your prompts. This might involve rephrasing the question, adding more detail, or simplifying complex language. Each tweak brings you closer to a prompt that extracts the ideal response, fostering a more productive interaction.

Feedback mechanisms embedded within ChatGPT serve as valuable tools for enhancing response quality. These tools allow you to rate responses, providing the AI with insights into what works and what doesn't. If you encounter inaccuracies, reporting them helps improve future interactions. By flagging errors, you contribute to refining the AI's understanding and performance. Additionally, suggesting corrections when you spot inaccuracies can aid in fine-tuning the system. This collaborative process not only benefits you but also enhances the AI's overall capability. Engaging with these feedback tools is akin to having a direct line of communication with the developers, enabling you to influence the evolution of ChatGPT in real time.

When you approach these challenges with patience and precision, you transform your interactions with ChatGPT from frustrating exchanges into rewarding dialogues. The key lies in understanding the nature of the tool and its potential limitations. By refining your prompts, utilizing feedback, and embracing an iterative mindset, you unlock a more intuitive and effective communication channel with the AI, paving the way for more accurate and relevant interactions.

7.2 ENSURING DATA PRIVACY AND SECURITY

Our digital world is immense and interconnected, with our personal data often strewn across multiple platforms. This makes safeguarding user information not just a priority but a necessity. Encrypting data is one of the most effective ways to protect it from unauthorized access. Encryption transforms your information into a coded format, decipherable only to those with the proper key. This ensures that even if data is intercepted, it remains unreadable to prying eyes. Another pillar of protection is the use of secure authentication methods. Think of it as a digital security guard verifying identities before granting access. This could involve multi-factor authentication, where you need more than just a password to log in, adding an extra layer of security to your accounts.

Configuring privacy settings in ChatGPT can significantly enhance your data protection. Start by adjusting data-sharing preferences. This means controlling what information you allow the service to access and share. For instance, you could limit data sharing to essential functions only, minimizing exposure. Anonymizing user inputs and outputs is another critical step. By ensuring your interactions with ChatGPT remain anonymous, you reduce the risk of personal information being linked back to you. This can be achieved by using pseudonyms or opting for settings that strip identifiable details from your inputs and responses.

Compliance with data protection regulations is crucial for main-taining trust and legal integrity. Regulations like the General Data Protection Regulation (GDPR) and the California Consumer Privacy Act (CCPA) set clear guidelines for how data should be handled. Understanding these regulations is the first step toward compliance. GDPR, for example, emphasizes user consent and the right to access personal data, while CCPA focuses on transparency and the right to opt out of data sales. Implementing necessary compliance measures involves aligning your data practices with these legal standards. This might include updating privacy poli-cies, ensuring data portability, and providing mechanisms for users to exercise their rights.

Educating users on privacy is not just about informing them of risks but empowering them to take control of their data. Sharing best prac-tices for data security can help users protect their information more effectively. For example, encourage using strong, unique passwords for different accounts and regularly updating these passwords. Discuss the importance of being cautious about the information shared online and recognizing phishing attempts. Encouraging regular reviews of privacy settings ensures that users remain aware of who has access to their data and can adjust permissions as necessary. This proactive approach fosters a culture of vigilance, where users are not passive participants but active defenders of their digital privacy.

Knowledge is power in navigating the complexities of digital privacy. Understanding these principles equips you to make informed decisions and safeguard your personal information in an increasingly interconnected world. It's about taking control and ensuring that your digital footprint remains secure and private. Active engagement with privacy settings and regulations, combined with a commitment to ongoing education, arms you with the tools needed to protect your data effectively.

7.3 MANAGING SYSTEM ERRORS AND GLITCHES

Navigating the digital world with ChatGPT can sometimes be like dealing with a moody appliance that works perfectly one day and acts up the next. Common system errors users might encounter include connection issues, API response errors, and unexpected system crashes. These glitches can disrupt your workflow, causing frustration and delays. Connection issues are often the culprits when the interface seems unresponsive or takes too long to load. This might be due to intermittent internet connectivity or server problems on OpenAI's end. API response errors, on the other hand, occur when the system struggles to process your requests, leading to incomplete or delayed outputs. You may find that responses are missing vital details or fail to load altogether. Unexpected system crashes are less common but can be disconcerting, often requiring a full restart of the application to restore functionality.

Following a step-by-step approach can be invaluable in tackling these issues head-on. First, check your internet connection. It might seem obvious, but often, a simple disconnect and reconnect can resolve many connectivity problems. Ensure your Wi-Fi signal is strong, or switch to a wired connection if possible. If you're dealing with API response errors, re-authenticating your API keys could help. This involves logging out of your account and logging back in or refreshing your API token if you're using ChatGPT in a developer setting. Should you experience a system crash, restarting the application is usually the first step. Close the app completely, wait a few moments, and then reopen it. This can clear temporary glitches and restore normal operations.

When faced with persistent issues, knowing where to seek support is crucial. OpenAI's support center is a treasure trove of resources designed to assist with troubleshooting and common queries. Here, you can find detailed guides and FAQs that cover a wide range of topics, from basic setup tips to advanced troubleshooting strategies. Additionally, user forums and community groups offer platforms for sharing experiences and solutions. Engaging with these communities can be incredibly helpful, as fellow users often provide insights or workarounds that aren't covered in official documentation. These forums act as collective brains, pooling knowledge to solve common problems. For on-the-go assistance, keep a list of troubleshooting guides handy. They can serve as quick references to address issues as they arise, minimizing down-time and ensuring a smoother experience.

Proactive measures can significantly reduce the frequency of these errors and glitches. Keeping your software up-to-date is a funda-mental step. Regular updates often include patches and improve-ments that address known bugs, enhancing overall stability. Make it a habit to check for updates regularly and install them promptly. Reviewing system logs can also provide insights into recurring issues. By examining these logs, you might identify patterns or specific triggers that lead to errors. Addressing these underlying causes can prevent future occurrences. Implementing robust error handling in API calls is another proactive strategy. This means designing your API requests to handle potential failures gracefully, ensuring that your application can recover quickly from disruptions. By incorporating these measures into your routine, you create a more resilient framework for using ChatGPT, minimizing interruptions, and maximizing productivity.

7.4 OPTIMIZING PERFORMANCE AND SPEED

Imagine you're in a bustling kitchen during dinner service. Every second counts and efficiency is key. Similarly, when using Chat-GPT, understanding performance metrics is vital for smooth and speedy interactions. Response time is one of the most critical metrics. It measures the time taken for ChatGPT to process your input and deliver a response. The shorter the response time, the more efficient the interaction. Throughput, another important metric, refers to the number of tasks the system can handle simultaneously. High throughput means ChatGPT can manage multiple requests without bottlenecking, just like a chef who can juggle several dishes at once. Latency, often confused with response time, specifically denotes the delay before the system starts processing your request. Reducing latency ensures that ChatGPT begins working on your input without unnecessary delays, making interactions feel more fluid and immediate.

To optimize ChatGPT's performance, configuring settings thoughtfully can make a significant difference. Allocating sufficient resources is akin to ensuring your kitchen has enough cooks. Make sure your system has the necessary computational power to handle ChatGPT's demands. This might involve upgrading hardware or ensuring that background applications aren't hogging resources. Configuring response time and processing power settings can also help. By adjusting these parameters, you tailor the system's performance to match your specific needs, whether you require quick, concise answers or more detailed, thoughtful responses. This customization allows ChatGPT to operate at its full potential, efficiently meeting your expectations.

Caching strategies are another way to boost performance, much like pre-preparing ingredients in a kitchen to speed up meal prep. Response caching involves storing frequently used responses to common queries, allowing ChatGPT to retrieve them quickly without recalculating each time. This is particularly useful for repetitive tasks or inquiries that don't require unique, real-time processing. Implementing data caching for frequently requested information serves a similar purpose. By keeping often-used data readily accessible, ChatGPT reduces the time spent re-fetching details, speeding up the overall interaction process. This approach not only enhances performance but also ensures that resources are used efficiently, minimizing unnecessary computation.

Regular performance monitoring is crucial to maintaining ChatGPT's efficiency, similar to checking the kitchen's workflow during service. Setting up performance dashboards provides a real-time overview of key metrics, allowing you to spot potential issues before they become problems. These dashboards act as a control center, offering insights into system performance and identifying areas for improvement. Using automated monitoring tools can further streamline this process. These tools continuously assess performance metrics, alerting you to anomalies or trends that might require attention. Analyzing performance data regularly enables you to make informed decisions about adjustments, whether it's tweaking configurations or scaling resources. Consistent monitoring ensures that ChatGPT remains responsive and efficient, ready to handle your queries with ease.

With these strategies in place, ChatGPT can operate seamlessly, transforming potential bottlenecks into free-flowing interactions. By understanding and optimizing performance metrics, you ensure that the system responds with the speed and accuracy you expect, enhancing the overall user experience. It's about creating an environment where ChatGPT can thrive, delivering reliable and efficient responses every time you engage with it.

7.5 STAYING UPDATED WITH CHATGPT DEVELOPMENTS

In a world where technology evolves at lightning speed, staying informed about the latest developments in ChatGPT is crucial. One effective way to stay in the loop is by subscribing to OpenAI newsletters. These newsletters are a direct line from the creators, offering insights into the latest updates, features, and even behind-the-scenes glimpses of what's coming next. They provide a curated source of information, ensuring you never miss out on crucial updates or enhancements that can impact how you use ChatGPT. Alongside newsletters, following OpenAI's official social media channels also keeps you connected. Platforms like Twitter and LinkedIn are often where OpenAI shares real-time announcements, tips, and community highlights. Engaging with these channels allows you to receive information as it happens, keeping you ahead of the curve.

Engaging with the community is not just about staying informed —it's about being part of a collective learning experience. Joining ChatGPT user groups can open doors to new perspectives and innovative ways to use the tool. These groups are often vibrant spaces where users share experiences, solutions, and creative applications of ChatGPT. Participating in discussions allows you to contribute your insights while learning from others, creating a dynamic exchange of knowledge. Whether you're troubleshooting an issue or exploring a new feature, community forums can offer invaluable support and inspiration. They are places where collective intelligence thrives, enabling users to learn from shared experiences and collaborate on finding solutions.

For those eager to deepen their understanding of ChatGPT and AI, accessing educational resources is a step in the right direction. Online courses and tutorials offer structured learning pathways, guiding you through both basic functionalities and advanced features. These courses are designed to cater to varying levels of expertise, ensuring that both beginners and more experienced users can find valuable content. Webinars and workshops provide interactive experiences, allowing you to engage with experts and ask questions in real time. They are opportunities to expand your knowledge and to hear firsthand from those at the forefront of AI development. Additionally, diving into research papers and publications can offer a more in-depth understanding of the theories and technologies that underpin ChatGPT. These resources are treasure troves of information, providing a deeper look into the innovations driving AI forward.

Testing new features is an exciting way to contribute to the development of ChatGPT. By signing up for beta testing programs, you gain early access to new functionalities and have the chance to shape their evolution. This involvement not only gives you a sneak peek into future updates but also allows you to provide constructive feedback directly to OpenAI. Your experiences and insights can influence how features are refined and implemented. Sharing these experiences with the community can further enhance the collective understanding of new tools and capabilities. It's a collaborative process where your input can lead to improvements that benefit all users.

As you navigate the evolving landscape of ChatGPT, these strategies can empower you to make the most of what this tool has to offer. Staying updated, engaging with the community, and continuously learning are keys to unlocking the full potential of ChatGPT. By embracing these practices, you position yourself to leverage the latest innovations and contribute to the ongoing dialogue around AI, ensuring that you remain at the forefront of technology's exciting developments.

CHAPTER 8
FUTURE TRENDS AND CONTINUOUS LEARNING

Picture a world where cars drive themselves, making traffic jams a relic of the past and freeing you to focus on more fulfilling pursuits during your commute. This isn't science fiction; it's an emerging reality, thanks to the rapid advancements in artificial intelligence. AI is revolutionizing industries at a pace that few could have imagined, and it's transforming how we interact with the world around us. As we stand on the cusp of this new era, understanding the potential trajectory of AI and its implications becomes crucial.

In the realm of autonomous vehicles, AI is poised to redefine transportation. Companies like Wayve are pioneering new approaches by integrating AI into vehicles, enabling them to navigate complex urban environments. These advancements promise increased efficiency and safety, reducing the need for human intervention in driving tasks. These systems learn from countless scenarios by utilizing generative AI and synthetic data, improving their decision-making capabilities. This evolution in autonomous driving not only holds the potential to reduce road accidents but also to reshape our urban landscapes by alleviating congestion and pollution.

Similarly, AI is making significant strides in healthcare diagnostics, promising early disease detection and personalized treatment plans. AI algorithms can analyze vast datasets to identify patterns and anomalies that might elude even the most skilled human practitioners. This capability enhances diagnostic accuracy, leading to more effective interventions and better patient outcomes. The integration of AI in healthcare does not replace the expertise of medical professionals but rather augments it, enabling a collaborative approach to patient care that leverages the strengths of both humans and machines.

In the education sector, AI is personalizing learning experiences and tailoring instruction to meet the unique needs of each student. By analyzing data on student performance, AI systems can identify areas where learners excel and those where they may need additional support. This individualized approach empowers educators to create more effective curricula and fosters an environment where students can thrive. As AI continues to evolve, its role in education is likely to expand, offering new opportunities for innovation and accessibility in learning.

The impact of AI extends beyond these sectors, promising to transform industries such as finance, retail, and manufacturing. In finance, AI-driven algorithms optimize trading strategies, manage risks, and detect fraudulent activities with unprecedented precision. Retailers utilize AI to enhance customer experiences, offering personalized recommendations and streamlining operations. Meanwhile, in manufacturing, AI improves supply chain management, predicting demand and optimizing production schedules to enhance efficiency and reduce waste.

As AI becomes more pervasive, ethical considerations take center stage. As automation takes over routine tasks, the potential for job displacement raises questions about the future workforce. It is crucial to develop strategies that mitigate these impacts, such as retraining programs and policies that support workers in transitioning to new roles. Additionally, ensuring unbiased AI systems is paramount. AI must reflect diverse perspectives and experiences to avoid perpetuating existing inequalities. Maintaining data privacy and security is another critical concern, as the vast amounts of information processed by AI systems must be protected against misuse.

AI also holds promise in addressing global challenges, such as climate change and disaster response. In climate change mitigation, AI analyzes environmental data to identify trends and develop sustainable solutions. This technology can optimize energy consumption, reduce emissions, and enhance resource management, contributing to a more sustainable future. During natural disasters, AI systems provide real-time data analysis, aiding in efficient resource allocation and improving emergency response efforts. In the realm of global health, AI supports initiatives by predicting disease outbreaks, optimizing vaccine distribution, and enhancing public health strategies.

Reflection Section: Imagining AI's Future in Your Life

Consider how AI advancements might shape your personal and professional life. Reflect on areas where AI could enhance your daily routines or solve challenges you face. How might these transformations impact your industry or community? What ethical considerations are most relevant to you, and how can you contribute to shaping a future where AI serves the greater good?

AI's potential to drive innovation and solve complex problems is immense as we look to the future. By understanding its capabilities and implications, we can harness its power responsibly and ethically, ensuring that its benefits are shared widely across society.

8.1 EMERGING TRENDS IN NATURAL LANGUAGE PROCESSING

Natural Language Processing (NLP) continues to evolve, driven by remarkable advances in technology and the increasing demand for machines that understand human language. At the forefront of these developments are transformer-based models, which have revolutionized how machines process language. Unlike their predecessors, these models excel at capturing long-range dependencies in text. This ability translates into a deeper understanding of context, resulting in more accurate and coherent responses. Transformers don't just stop there. They also introduce the concept of contextual embeddings, where the words around it influence the meaning of a word. This nuanced understanding allows for richer interpretations, enabling AI systems to grasp subtleties that were previously out of reach.

Zero-shot learning is another exciting advancement in NLP. This approach allows models to make predictions about tasks they have yet to be explicitly trained on. Imagine teaching a child to recognize apples and then asking them to identify oranges without prior exposure. Zero-shot learning empowers AI to make such leaps, broadening its applicability across various tasks with minimal additional training. This capability is particularly impactful in dynamic environments, where the ability to adapt quickly is crucial.

As the world becomes more interconnected, the importance of NLP in multilingual contexts grows. Translation systems are evolving, becoming more sophisticated in their ability to bridge language barriers. These systems don't just convert words; they capture the essence of meaning, ensuring that translations remain true to the original intent. Cross-lingual information retrieval is another area where NLP shines. It enables users to search for information in one language and receive results in another, opening up access to global knowledge. Multilingual chatbots are becoming common, allowing businesses to reach diverse audiences by providing seamless communication across languages. These advancements make the world smaller and more connected, fostering understanding and collaboration on a global scale.

Conversational AI is undergoing a transformation, driven by a desire for more natural and intuitive interactions. Context-aware chatbots are leading this charge, capable of remembering previous interactions and using that information to inform current conversations. This continuity creates a more personalized experience, akin to speaking with a friend who knows your history. Emotionally intelligent AI is also emerging, with systems that can detect and respond to human emotions. This capability adds a layer of empathy to interactions, allowing AI to tailor its responses based on the user's emotional state. Voice-activated assistants are becoming more sophisticated, offering hands-free convenience and accessibility. They are learning to understand not just words but the nuances of tone and intention, making interactions smoother and more effective.

NLP is also playing a crucial role in enhancing accessibility for diverse user groups. Text-to-speech technology transforms written content into spoken words, making information accessible to individuals with visual impairments. This technology also supports those who prefer auditory learning, offering an alternative way to consume information. Speech-to-text applications are equally transformative, converting spoken language into written text. This capability benefits individuals with hearing impairments and those who find typing challenging. Assistive AI is emerging as a powerful tool for individuals with disabilities, offering tailored support that enhances independence and participation in everyday activities. By addressing diverse needs, NLP-driven technologies are creating a more inclusive digital landscape where everyone can engage and thrive.

8.2 EXPLORING NEW FEATURES AND UPDATES

In recent times, ChatGPT has seen some exciting updates that enhance its functionality and user experience. One of the standout improvements is in response accuracy. The developers have fine-tuned the model, enabling it to understand the nuances of human language better, which results in more precise and relevant replies. This adjustment is particularly beneficial when you engage the AI for complex queries or when you need detailed information. Alongside this, the user interface has undergone a facelift, making it more intuitive and user-friendly. The streamlined design not only looks appealing but also facilitates smoother navigation, allowing you to focus on your tasks without unnecessary distractions. Moreover, new API capabilities have been introduced. These allow developers to integrate ChatGPT more seamlessly into various applications, broadening its usability across different platforms and enhancing the potential for personalized automation.

Looking ahead, several promising features are in the pipeline that promise to elevate ChatGPT's capabilities even further. One such feature is real-time collaboration tools. Imagine being able to work alongside ChatGPT while it assists you in drafting documents or brainstorming ideas, all in real time. This functionality will enable smoother and more interactive workflows, especially in team settings. AI-driven analytics is another exciting development. By leveraging data more effectively, ChatGPT will offer insights and analytics that can inform decision-making processes, providing users with actionable information. Additionally, advanced person-alization options are set to redefine user interaction. These features will tailor responses based on user history and preferences, offering an experience that feels uniquely catered to each individual.

User feedback plays a crucial role in shaping these updates and future developments. OpenAI actively solicits feedback and analyzes it to identify common themes and areas for improve-ment. This feedback loop ensures that the features being devel-oped align with user needs and expectations. By prioritizing feature requests, the developers can focus on enhancements that will have the most significant impact. Implementing user-suggested improvements not only refines the platform but also fosters a sense of community where users feel their voices are heard and valued. This collaborative approach is essential in main-taining a cutting-edge tool that evolves with its user base.

For those eager to explore these updates before they become widely available, beta testing and early access programs offer a unique opportunity. By signing up for these programs, you gain early access to the latest features, allowing you to test them in your environment. This can be particularly advantageous for power users or developers looking to integrate new functionalities into their projects. Providing feedback during this phase is invaluable, as it helps refine the features, ensuring they meet user expectations upon release. Early access not only gives you a competitive edge by staying ahead of the curve but also allows you to shape the devel-opment of the tools you rely on. Engaging with these programs is not just about getting a sneak peek; it's about being part of a collaborative effort to push the boundaries of what's possible with AI.

8.3 LEARNING FROM AI EXPERTS AND THOUGHT LEADERS

Engaging with AI thought leaders offers a unique window into the minds driving this transformative field. These individuals are not only at the forefront of technological advancements but are also shaping the conversation around the ethical and practical implications of AI. Andrew Ng, a pioneer in machine learning, co-founded Coursera and has played pivotal roles in projects like Google Brain. His insights into AI and education are invaluable for anyone eager to understand the intersection of these domains. Similarly, Demis Hassabis, the founder of DeepMind, has made groundbreaking contributions through projects like AlphaGo. His work exemplifies the potential of AI to tackle complex challenges. Fei-Fei Li's research in computer vision and AI in healthcare highlights the importance of human-centered AI, making her a key figure to follow for those interested in the societal impact of technology. These experts, along with others like Geoffrey Hinton and Yann LeCun, regularly share their findings and perspectives, offering a wealth of knowledge to those who seek to deepen their understanding of AI.

Attending AI conferences and seminars is another way to immerse yourself in the latest developments and network with professionals in the field. Events like the AI Summit and NeurIPS (Conference on Neural Information Processing Systems) attract thousands of attendees, including leading researchers and industry professionals. These gatherings provide opportunities to hear keynote presentations, participate in panel discussions, and engage in workshops that cover a wide range of topics. At the ICML (International Conference on Machine Learning), you can explore cutting-edge research and applications in machine learning, gaining insights into the methods and tools that are shaping the future of AI. These conferences are not just about learning; they're about connecting with a community of innovators who are passionate about advancing the field. The exchange of ideas and perspectives at these events fosters collaboration and inspires new approaches to solving complex problems.

For those who prefer a more flexible approach to learning, webinars and online courses offer a convenient way to stay informed about AI. Platforms like Coursera provide a range of AI courses, from introductory classes to advanced specializations. These courses, often led by top university professors and industry experts, allow you to learn at your own pace while gaining a solid foundation in AI principles. MIT also offers online programs that delve into the intricacies of AI, providing a rigorous academic perspective. OpenAI hosts webinars that cover various aspects of AI development and application, offering insights directly from the creators of some of the most advanced AI models. These resources are invaluable for anyone looking to expand their knowledge and skills, providing the tools needed to engage with AI more effectively.

AI research papers and journals are essential for keeping up with the latest findings and breakthroughs in the field. The Journal of Artificial Intelligence Research (JAIR) publishes high-quality articles that span the breadth of AI, from theoretical foundations to practical applications. Reading through these papers can deepen your understanding of the methodologies and technologies driving AI innovation. The Proceedings of the AAAI Conference on Artificial Intelligence is another critical resource, offering peer-reviewed papers showcasing recent research and trends. For those interested in the bleeding edge of AI, arXiv provides access to preprints of new research, allowing you to explore emerging ideas before they are formally published. Engaging with these publications challenges you to think critically about AI and its implications, equipping you with the knowledge to contribute to the ongoing conversation around its development and use.

8.4 COMMUNITY AND SUPPORT RESOURCES

Discovering and participating in online AI communities can significantly enhance your understanding and engagement with artificial intelligence. These digital spaces connect you with like-minded individuals who share a passion for AI and machine learning. For instance, the Reddit AI and Machine Learning communities offer platforms where enthusiasts and experts alike discuss the latest developments, share resources, and troubleshoot challenges. These forums are bustling with activity, where questions about AI algorithms, coding challenges, or ethical considerations are met with diverse insights. Similarly, LinkedIn hosts various AI discussion groups, providing a professional setting where industry leaders and newcomers exchange ideas, debate trends, and build valuable connections. These groups are excellent for networking and staying updated on industry news. AI forums and subreddits serve as informal hubs where you can dive into technical discussions or explore broader topics like the societal impact of AI, making them a valuable resource for both learning and interaction.

Support groups and forums are invaluable when you need advice or troubleshooting assistance. The OpenAI Community Forum is a dedicated space for users to seek help, share experiences, and collaborate on projects related to AI. It's a place where you can find answers to your questions, whether you're facing technical issues or seeking guidance on best practices. Stack Overflow, known for its vast repository of coding and tech-related queries, is a go-to for AI-related questions. Here, developers and AI practitioners share solutions to common programming challenges, making it a vital tool for overcoming obstacles in your AI projects. Discord also hosts numerous AI user groups, offering real-time communication with fellow AI enthusiasts. These groups facilitate direct interaction, allowing for quick exchanges of ideas and solutions, which can be particularly beneficial for those who prefer instant feedback and collaboration.

Mentorship and networking opportunities in the AI field can significantly accelerate your growth and understanding. AI mentorship programs pair you with experienced professionals who provide guidance, share their expertise, and help you navigate the complexities of the field. These relationships can open doors to insights and career opportunities that might otherwise remain out of reach. Networking events and meetups offer more informal settings to connect with peers and industry leaders. These gatherings provide a platform for discussing recent advancements, exchanging ideas, and forming collaborations. AI hackathons and competitions are exciting venues for applying your skills in real-world scenarios. They challenge you to solve complex problems, often under time constraints, promoting innovation and teamwork. These events hone your technical abilities and expand your professional network, making them an excellent opportunity for personal and career development.

Contributing to the AI community is not just about receiving knowledge but also sharing it. By engaging actively, you can help shape the future of AI. Sharing your knowledge and insights, whether through blog posts, tutorials, or discussions, enriches the community and fosters a culture of continuous learning. Participating in open-source AI projects is another impactful way to contribute. These projects welcome developers of all skill levels and provide a collaborative environment for building and refining

AI tools. Your contributions, no matter how small, can lead to significant advancements and innovations. Writing and publishing AI-related content, such as articles or research papers, is another way to leave your mark. It allows you to present your ideas and findings to a broader audience, sparking conversations and inspiring others in the field. Engaging with the AI community in these ways not only enhances your knowledge and skills but also strengthens the collective wisdom and progress of the field.

8.5 BUILDING A LIFELONG LEARNING PLAN FOR AI AND CHATGPT

Creating a lifelong learning plan for AI and ChatGPT starts with setting clear, realistic goals. Begin by identifying the AI topics that pique your interest. This could range from natural language processing to the ethical considerations of AI in society. Once you've pinpointed these areas, set both short-term and long-term objectives. Short-term goals might include completing an introductory course on AI or experimenting with ChatGPT to understand its capabilities. Long-term goals involve mastering a programming language commonly used in AI, such as Python, or contributing to open-source AI projects. Establishing a timeline for these goals can keep you on track. Allocate time each week or month to focus on these objectives, and adjust your schedule as needed to accommodate new interests or changes in your availability.

Curating your learning resources is another crucial step. The internet brims with courses and tutorials tailored to various learning styles and levels. Websites like Coursera and edX offer structured courses, while platforms like YouTube provide free, accessible tutorials. Selecting relevant books and research papers can deepen your understanding. Look for works by respected authors in the field or browse academic journals for the latest research findings. Following AI blogs and podcasts can keep you informed about trends and innovations. Blogs often provide insights from industry leaders, while podcasts allow you to absorb information during commutes or while multitasking. Tailor your resource list to align with your goals and interests, ensuring it evolves as your understanding deepens.

Keeping your knowledge up-to-date is vital in the fast-paced world of AI. Schedule regular study sessions to review the latest developments and explore new topics. This consistent engagement helps solidify your understanding and keeps you from falling behind. Attending AI webinars and workshops can provide fresh perspectives and practical insights. These events often feature experts sharing their experiences and offering advice on applying AI in real-world scenarios. Engaging with the latest AI research can also be enlightening. Reading research papers or attending conferences exposes you to cutting-edge innovations and encourages critical thinking. By staying informed, you position yourself to adapt to new challenges and opportunities in the AI landscape.

Evaluating your progress is essential in maintaining motivation and ensuring your learning plan remains effective. Set milestones to track your achievements and celebrate your successes. Whether it's completing a course or successfully implementing a new AI tool, acknowledging these accomplishments can boost your confidence. Reflect on your learning experiences to identify areas of strength and those requiring further attention. This reflection can guide you in adjusting your learning plans as needed. Perhaps a particular topic has sparked a new interest, or maybe you've encountered unexpected challenges that necessitate a shift in focus. Being open to adapting your plan keeps your learning journey dynamic and aligned with your evolving goals and interests.

In wrapping up this chapter, remember that lifelong learning in AI and ChatGPT is a continuous process. It requires curiosity, commitment, and a willingness to adapt. By setting goals, curating resources, staying updated, and evaluating progress, you lay a solid foundation for growth. This approach not only enhances your understanding of AI but also equips you to navigate an ever-changing technological landscape.

CONCLUSION

As we reach the end of this journey together, I want to reaffirm the vision and purpose that guided us from the very first page. This book was crafted with one goal in mind: to make ChatGPT accessible, understandable, and useful for beginners across various fields. Whether you're stepping into the world of technology for the first time or seeking to enhance your existing skills, my aim has been to provide you with a comprehensive yet approachable guide to harnessing the power of ChatGPT.

We began by exploring what ChatGPT is and how it can revolutionize everyday interactions. From setting up your account to navigating its interface, you were equipped with the foundational skills necessary to start using this tool effectively. We delved into the art of writing effective prompts and understanding how to communicate with ChatGPT to receive precise and relevant responses. This core skill is vital, as it forms the basis of all interactions with the AI.

In subsequent chapters, we explored practical applications across personal productivity, professional use, and creative endeavors. You learned how ChatGPT can assist in organizing tasks, drafting emails, and even creating art or music. Each example demonstrated the versatility of ChatGPT, showing how it can seamlessly integrate into various aspects of your life.

As we ventured into advanced features and customization, you discovered ways to tailor your ChatGPT experience to suit your personal preferences and professional needs. We discussed API integration, memory capabilities, and even how to create custom chatbot personalities. These tools empower you to extend ChatGPT's functionalities beyond the basics, opening new possibilities for innovation and efficiency.

We also addressed the challenges and ethical considerations associated with AI usage. You were encouraged to think critically about AI's ethical implications, including data privacy and bias. Understanding these concerns helps ensure that your use of ChatGPT is responsible and aligned with ethical standards.

Throughout this book, the key takeaway is that ChatGPT is a tool of immense potential. It is capable of transforming how you work, learn, and create. But like any tool, its effectiveness hinges on how you use it. By crafting clear prompts, experimenting with its features, and applying it thoughtfully across domains, you can unlock its full potential.

Now, I urge you to take what you've learned and apply it. Experiment with ChatGPT in new ways, push its boundaries and explore its capabilities. Whether you're using it to streamline work processes, create art, or learn something new, continue to engage with it actively. The world of AI is constantly evolving, and staying curious and open to learning will keep you at the forefront of these advancements.

Let this book be a stepping stone in your journey with AI. Use it as a reference and a source of inspiration. Remember that learning is an ongoing process, and your interaction with ChatGPT can evolve as you do. Embrace the possibilities and let your creativity guide you. The future with AI is bright and full of potential, and I am excited for the opportunities that lie ahead for you.

Thank you for allowing me to guide you through this journey. I hope it has been as enlightening for you as it has been fulfilling for me to share. Together, let us continue to explore, innovate, and make the most of what technology has to offer.

KEEPING THE JOURNEY GOING

Now that you have all the tools to master ChatGPT with ease, it's your turn to share what you've learned and guide others to the same help.

By leaving a review on Amazon, you'll help other curious minds find *Master ChatGPT Effortlessly* and discover how to make the most of this amazing tool. Your honest thoughts will guide them on their path to confidence and creativity with ChatGPT.

Thank you for your support. When we share what we've learned, we keep the excitement of discovery alive—and you're helping me do just that.

Scan and share what you've learned!

REFERENCES

CapTech University. (n.d.). *The ethical considerations of artificial intelligence.* https://www.captechu.edu/blog/ethical-considerations-of-artificial-intelligence

Canda, J. (2024, October 1). *5 common generative AI prompt writing mistakes (and how to fix them).* Forbes. https://www.forbes.com/sites/bernardmarr/2024/10/01/5-common-generative-ai-prompt-writing-mistakes-and-how-to-fix-them/

Cook, J. (2023, June 26). *How to write effective prompts for ChatGPT: 7 essential steps for best results.* Forbes. https://www.forbes.com/sites/jodiecook/2023/06/26/how-to-write-effective-prompts-for-chatgpt-7-essential-steps-for-best-results/

Copy.ai. (n.d.). *AI for content creation: How to get started (& scale).* https://www.copy.ai/blog/ai-content-creation

Day Optimizer. (n.d.). *How to use ChatGPT to organize your tasks.* https://dayoptimizer.com/task-management/how-to-use-chatgpt-to-organize-your-tasks/

Hootsuite. (n.d.). *How to use ChatGPT for social media: Expert tips + 75 examples.* https://blog.hootsuite.com/chatgpt-social-media/

Harvard Gazette. (2020, October). *Ethical concerns mount as AI takes bigger decision-making role.* https://news.harvard.edu/gazette/story/2020/10/ethical-concerns-mount-as-ai-takes-bigger-decision-making-role/

Innodata. (n.d.). *Best approaches to mitigate bias in AI models.* https://innodata.com/best-approaches-to-mitigate-bias-in-ai-models/

Marr, B. (2024, March 3). *ChatGPT: A game-changer in game development. IFS Blog.* https://blog.ifs.com/2024/03/chatgpt-a-game-changer-in-game-development/#:

Medium. (2024, October 1). *AI in music: Composition, production, and recommendation.* https://medium.com/@jam.canda/ai-in-music-composition-production-and-recommendation-4b5bbde1b10b

Microsoft. (n.d.). *How to write poetry using Copilot.* https://www.microsoft.com/en-us/bing/do-more-with-ai/write-poetry-with-bing-compose?form=MA13KP

OpenAI. (n.d.). *Quickstart tutorial - OpenAI API.* https://platform.openai.com/docs/quickstart

OpenAI. (n.d.). *Custom instructions for ChatGPT.* https://openai.com/index/custom-instructions-for-chatgpt/

Persona Talent. (n.d.). *19 ways to use ChatGPT to boost your productivity.* https://www.personatalent.com/productivity/ways-to-use-chatgpt-to-boost-your-productivity/

Salesforce. (n.d.). *Everything you need to know about AI in customer service.* https://www.salesforce.com/service/ai/customer-service-ai/

Scott, A. (2023, May 29). *The integration of ChatGPT in smart homes: Voice-activated home automation.* https://scottamyx.com/2023/05/29/the-integration-of-chatgpt-in-smart-homes-voice-activated-home-automation/

Search Engine Land. (n.d.). *ChatGPT fails: 13 common errors and mistakes you need to know.* https://searchengineland.com/chatgpt-fails-errors-mistakes-400153

Technology Review. (2023, March 3). *The inside story of how ChatGPT was built from the people who made it.* https://www.technologyreview.com/2023/03/03/1069311/inside-story-oral-history-how-chatgpt-built-openai/

Tipalti. (n.d.). *ChatGPT for finance: 12 powerful uses.* https://tipalti.com/blog/chatgpt-for-finance/

Towards Data Science. (2020, October 2). *Transformers in NLP: A beginner friendly explanation.* https://towardsdatascience.com/transformers-89034557de14

WikiHow. (n.d.). *How to create a ChatGPT account: 8 steps (with pictures).* https://www.wikihow.com/Create-a-ChatGPT-Account

WordStream. (2023, March 6). *6 ways to use ChatGPT for small business marketing (+6 more tips).* https://www.wordstream.com/blog/ws/2023/03/06/how-to-use-chatgpt-for-small-business-marketing

ZDNet. (n.d.). *7 advanced ChatGPT prompt-writing tips you need to know.* https://www.zdnet.com/article/7-advanced-chatgpt-prompt-writing-tips-you-need-to-know/

Anodot. (n.d.). *Top 10 thought leaders in AI/ML we're following.* https://www.anodot.com/blog/top-10-thought-leaders-in-aiml/

Forbes. (2023, February 20). *Top AI conferences 2023: Roundup of top AI conferences.* https://www.forbes.com/sites/qai/2023/02/20/top-ai-conferences-2023-roundup-of-top-ai-conferences/

Atlassian. (n.d.). *AI for project management: Tools and best practices.* https://www.atlassian.com/work-management/project-management/ai-project-management

CSIS. (n.d.). *Protecting data privacy as a baseline for responsible AI.* https://www.csis.org/analysis/protecting-data-privacy-baseline-responsible-ai

Medium. (2024, September 15). *Emerging trends in the future of natural language processing.* https://medium.com/@faaiz.ul.haq3333/emerging-trends-in-the-future-of-natural-language-processing-62aee94630ac

Made in the USA
Middletown, DE
29 March 2025

73467985R00072